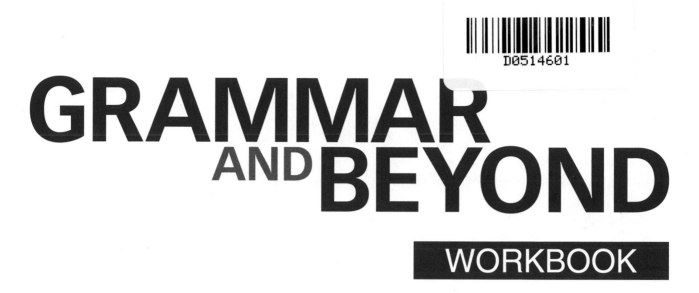

GRAMMAR AND BEYOND

WORKBOOK

Laurie Blass
Barbara Denman
Susan Iannuzzi

4B

CAMBRIDGE
UNIVERSITY PRESS

CAMBRIDGE UNIVERSITY PRESS
Cambridge, New York, Melbourne, Madrid, Cape Town,
Singapore, São Paulo, Delhi, Mexico City

Cambridge University Press
32 Avenue of the Americas, New York, NY 10013-2473, USA

www.cambridge.org
Information on this title: www.cambridge.org/9781107604117

First published 2013
2nd printing 2013

Printed in the United States of America

A catalog record for this publication is available from the British Library.

ISBN 978-0-521-14301-1 Student's Book 4
ISBN 978-0-521-14323-3 Student's Book 4A
ISBN 978-0-521-14328-8 Student's Book 4B
ISBN 978-1-107-60409-4 Workbook 4
ISBN 978-1-107-60410-0 Workbook 4A
ISBN 978-1-107-60411-7 Workbook 4B
ISBN 978-1-107-67297-0 Teacher Support Resource Book with CD-ROM 4
ISBN 978-0-521-14343-1 Class Audio CD 4
ISBN 978-1-139-06188-9 Writing Skills Interactive 4

Art direction and layout services: Integra
Editorial management: Hyphen S.A.

Contents

PART 4 Classification and Definition | Business

UNIT 11 Classification and Definition 1 Job Interviews   94
The Passive   94
Common Words and Phrases Used in Classification Writing   99
Avoid Common Mistakes   101
Self-Assessment   102

UNIT 12 Classification and Definition 2 Your Ideal Job   104
The Language of Definition   104
Appositives   107
Avoid Common Mistakes   111
Self-Assessment   112

PART 5 Problem–Solution | Nutrition and Health

UNIT 13 Problem–Solution 1 Food and Technology   114
Present Perfect and Present Perfect Progressive   114
Common Noun Phrase Structures   118
Avoid Common Mistakes   121
Self-Assessment   122

UNIT 14 Problem–Solution 2 Children and Health   124
Reporting Verbs   124
Adverb Clauses and Phrases with *As*   126
Common Vocabulary for Describing Information in Graphics   128
Avoid Common Mistakes   129
Self-Assessment   130

UNIT 15 Problem–Solution 3 Health and Technology   132
Adverb Clauses of Purpose and Infinitives of Purpose   132
Reducing Adverb Clauses to Phrases   135
Common Vocabulary to Describe Problems and Solutions   137
Avoid Common Mistakes   138
Self-Assessment   140

UNIT **16** **Problem–Solution 4** Leading a Healthy Life   **142**

    It Constructions   **142**

    Common Transition Words to Indicate Steps of a Solution   **145**

    Avoid Common Mistakes   **147**

    Self-Assessment   **148**

PART 6 Summary–Response and Persuasion | Social Issues and Technology

UNIT **17** **Summary–Response** Privacy in the Digital Age   **150**

    Past Unreal Conditionals   **150**

    Common Phrases Used in Summary–Response Writing   **154**

    Avoid Common Mistakes   **155**

    Self-Assessment   **156**

UNIT **18** **Persuasion 1** Violence in the Media   **158**

    Nonidentifying Relative Clauses in Persuasive Writing   **158**

    Phrases That Limit Overgeneralization   **161**

    Avoid Common Mistakes   **163**

    Self-Assessment   **164**

UNIT **19** **Persuasion 2** Living in an Age of Information Overload   **166**

    Noun Clauses with *Wh-* Words and *If / Whether*   **166**

    Phrases for Argumentation   **169**

    Avoid Common Mistakes   **171**

    Self-Assessment   **172**

UNIT **20** **Persuasion 3** Social Networking   **174**

    Expressing Future Actions   **174**

    Common Words and Phrases in Persuasive Writing   **176**

    Avoid Common Mistakes   **178**

    Self-Assessment   **180**

Art Credits

Illustration

Bill Dickson: 151; **Rob Schuster:** 4; **Matt Stevens:** 96;
Richard Williams: 49, 104

Photography

6 ©Jonio Machado/Age Fotostock; 13 ©iStockphoto/Thinkstock; 19 ©Vladimir Godnik/Getty Images; 30 ©Martin San/Stone/Getty Images; 36 ©Palmi Gudmundsson/Nordic Photos/Getty Images; 39 ©Paul Williams/Alamy; 44 ©Medioimages/Photodisc/Getty Images; 55 ©Ghislain & Marie Davi/Cultura/ Age Fotostock; 56 ©Ilya Terentyev/Vetta/Getty Images; 60 ©Lance King/ Getty Images Sport/Getty Images; 66 ©Jeremy Woodhouse/Blend Images/ Getty Images; 72 ©Redchopsticks/Getty Images; 78 ©Don Cravens/Time & Life Pictures/Getty Images; 79 *(all)* ©Time Life Pictures/Getty Images; 80 ©Hulton Collection/Getty Images; 86 ©PhotoQuest/Archive Photos/Getty Images; 90 ©DreamPictures/The Image Bank/Getty Images; 94 ©Commercial Eye/ Stockbyte/Getty Images; 109 ©Zero Creatives/Cultura/Getty Images; 110 ©Eric Audras/PhotoAlto Agency RF Collections/Getty Images; 115 ©Thomas Kitchin & Victoria Hurst/First Light/Getty Images; 116 ©Dinodia Photos/Alamy; 117 ©Fuse/Getty Images; 120 ©Mark Andersen/Rubberball/Getty Images; 124 ©Stockbyte/Getty Images; 132 ©Radius Images/Alamy; 134 ©Larry Williams/ Blend Images/Getty Images; 138 ©Richard Green/Commercial/Alamy; 143 ©Michael Rosenfeld/Getty Images; 153 ©Photodisc/Thinkstock; 175 ©Chris Ryan/OJO Images/Getty Images; 177 ©SimoJarratt/Corbis Super RF/Alamy

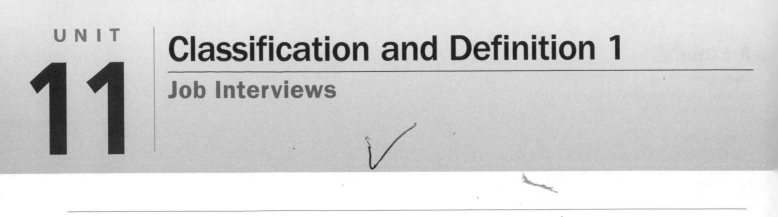

The Passive

1 Read the sentences about Nicholas's job interview. Then label each sentence.

AS = active sentence	PS = passive sentence

1. _AS_ Nicholas had a job interview last week at a small company not too far from his home.

2. _AS_ The company had advertised for an office assistant; Nicholas had some experience in an office.

3. _PS_ The application had to be submitted online.

4. _PS_ About two weeks later, Nicholas was called in for an interview at the company's main location.

5. _AS_ He felt nervous because he didn't know what to expect.

6. _PS_ He was greeted by the office manager and asked to sit in the conference room.

7. _PS_ The interview was conducted by a panel of three employees.

8. _AS_ After he'd responded to all of their questions, Nicholas had a chance to ask some questions of his own.

9. _PS_ Then he was given a short tour of the office.

10. _PS_ Nicholas was told that he would be contacted within a week.

11. _AC_ Despite his initial nervousness, Nicholas felt that the interview had gone well.

12. _PS_ Yesterday, Nicholas was offered the position.

2 Complete the sentences about filling job openings. Circle the word or phrase that correctly completes each sentence.

1. This is the process used when job openings _____ at the college where I work.

   (a.) are filled   b. fill   c. is filled

2. When a position is open or available, the first thing that happens is that the position _____ online.

   a. are advertised   (b.) is advertised   c. was advertised

3. It _____ to the newspaper, too, if it's a high-level position.

   (a.) may be sent   b. may send   c. sends

4. Some positions _____ as "Internal Candidates Only"; that means there are enough good candidates already working at the college.

   (a.) are classified   b. classified   c. classify

5. These positions _____ to non-employees.

   a. not offered   b. is being offered   (c.) will not be offered

6. After a position _____ as "open" for two weeks, it is closed.

   a. was listed   (b.) has been listed   c. lists

7. At that point, no more applications _____ .

   (a.) are accepted   b. accepted   c. is accepted

8. Then all of the applications _____ by a review committee; the committee eliminates any applicants who are not qualified.

   a. evaluated   b. is evaluated   (c.) are evaluated

9. The highest-rated applicants _____ to interview, usually with a panel of four or five employees.

   (a.) are invited   b. invited   c. to be invited

10. Once all of the interviews _____ , the panel recommends its top choices to the supervisor.

    a. have held   b. was being held   (c.) have been held

11. The best applicant _____ .

    (a.) is selected   b. selected   c. has been selected

12. Finally, he or she _____ the position.

    a. offers   (b.) is offered   c. is being offered

3 Complete the sentences about performance-based interviews. Circle the phrase that best completes each sentence.

1. An interview in which candidates are asked about their past behavior

   a. is referred to as a performance-based interview.

   b. refers to a performance-based interview.

   c. is being referred to as a performance-based interview.

2. Performance-based interviewing is based on the fact that past behavior

   a. can't be shown to be the best predictor of future behavior.

   b. should have been shown to be the best predictor of future behavior.

   c. has been shown to be the best predictor of future behavior.

3. A performance-based interview is structured so that examples of past behavior

   a. is elicited.

   b. can be elicited.

   c. may have been elicited.

4. In a performance-based interview, the applicant

   a. is asked to describe what he or she has done in a specific situation.

   b. described what he or she has done in a specific situation.

   c. is describing what he or she has done in a specific situation.

5. With the types of questions that are used in a performance-based interview, interviewees

   a. are asked to discuss their experiences, not their ideas.

   b. had discussed their experiences, not their ideas.

   c. had been required to discuss their experiences, not their ideas.

6. In this type of interview, most of the talking

   a. has been done by the applicant.

   b. was done by the applicant.

   c. is done by the applicant.

7. The difference between this kind of interview and a more traditional one

   a. can illustrate the type of answers each one requires.

   b. can be illustrated by the type of answers each one requires.

   c. could have been illustrated by the type of answers each one requires.

8. For instance, instead of the question, "How would you interact with an upset co-worker?" the question, "Tell me about a time when you had to interact with an upset co-worker"

   a. should have been included.

   b. was included.

   c. would be included.

9. Traditional methods choose candidates based on what they say they *would* do; better results

   a. can be obtained by asking candidates what they have actually done.

   b. had been obtained by asking candidates what they have actually done.

   c. ask candidates what they have actually done.

10. Moreover, in a performance-based interview, the potential employee

    a. gives a more accurate picture of the duties involved in the job.

    b. is given a more accurate picture of the duties involved in the job.

    c. was being given a more accurate picture of the duties involved in the job.

4 Rewrite the job interview guidelines using the passive form.

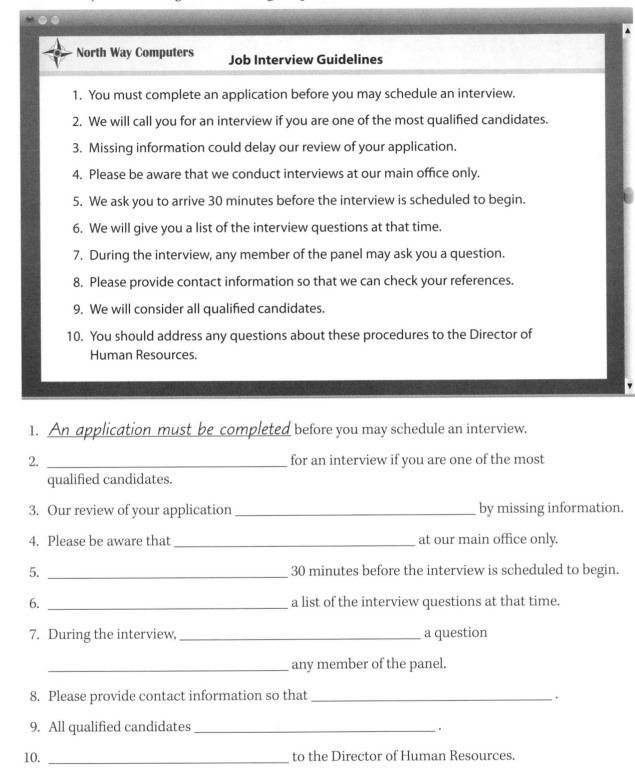

North Way Computers   **Job Interview Guidelines**

1. You must complete an application before you may schedule an interview.
2. We will call you for an interview if you are one of the most qualified candidates.
3. Missing information could delay our review of your application.
4. Please be aware that we conduct interviews at our main office only.
5. We ask you to arrive 30 minutes before the interview is scheduled to begin.
6. We will give you a list of the interview questions at that time.
7. During the interview, any member of the panel may ask you a question.
8. Please provide contact information so that we can check your references.
9. We will consider all qualified candidates.
10. You should address any questions about these procedures to the Director of Human Resources.

1. *An application must be completed* before you may schedule an interview.

2. _____ for an interview if you are one of the most qualified candidates.

3. Our review of your application _____ by missing information.

4. Please be aware that _____ at our main office only.

5. _____ 30 minutes before the interview is scheduled to begin.

6. _____ a list of the interview questions at that time.

7. During the interview, _____ a question _____ any member of the panel.

8. Please provide contact information so that _____ .

9. All qualified candidates _____ .

10. _____ to the Director of Human Resources.

5 Complete the article about studies on interviews. Use the correct form of the words in the box.

| analyze | argue | associate | be | ~~carry out~~ | compare | link | observe |

Studies that have been _carried out_ on interviewing have produced some interesting
                                    (1)

results, from a legal point of view. When data have _____ , clear lessons
                                                              (2)

have sometimes emerged. One example is a comparison of common interview formats.

When unstructured interviews were _____ to structured interviews, they
                                            (3)

_____ found to produce less consistent results. That is, unstructured interviews
        (4)

are _____ with wider variations in panel members' opinions. Thus, it can
          (5)

_____ that rigidly following a set of questions leaves hiring decisions less open
        (6)

to a legal challenge.

Another issue is how interviewer's recommendations are _____ to their
                                                                  (7)

feelings about candidates. It has _____ that some interviewers favor applicants
                                          (8)

who seem most like themselves. This behavior also must be avoided if the interview process

is to be fair and open.

Common Words and Phrases Used in Classification Writing

1 Complete the sentences about community colleges. Match the phrases to correctly complete
each sentence.

1. Community colleges often offer two types of programs: _b_ .

2. Depending on a student's goals, _____ .

3. Some colleges are able to offer part-time employment to their students, usually in _____ .

4. Services available at many colleges include both _____ .

5. A college's career center can provide assistance in a number of areas, _____ .

6. The advantages of working part-time while in college _____ .

a. clerical positions, library positions, and food service positions

b. credit and non-credit

c. including help with résumé writing and with job hunting

d. tutoring with academic subjects and career support services

e. include gaining job experience and learning new skills

f. a college can offer a number of options

2 Complete the sentences about organizational structures. Circle the phrase that best completes each sentence.

1. Most organizations have a structure that divides their employees into departments, and employees are assigned tasks _____ to their department.

    (a.)according   b. based   c. depending

2. In large organizations, each employment area or division is named _____ of the work it does, such as accounting, sales, and human resources.

    a. based   b. according   c. on the basis

3. The human resources department normally handles a _____ of functions related to employees and employment.

    a. consists   b. combination   c. basis

4. Most organizations also divide employees into groups _____ to their level of responsibility.

    a. according   b. based   c. depending

5. Depending on the level of each one's position, employees can be _____ employment categories.

    a. divided   b. divided into   c. divide

6. Each employment category can be _____ several levels of positions.

    a. consist of   b. involve   c. made up of

7. Job titles are assigned to positions _____ the duties and tasks the position requires.

    a. based on   b. on the basis   c. consisting of

8. Rates of pay can be at different levels, _____ how long the individual has worked for the company.

    a. depending on   b. on the basis   c. divided into

9. Experts recommend researching industry standards of pay and responsibility before going to an interview, _____ the type of job you are interviewing for.

    a. based on   b. is composed of   c. is divided into

10. Preparing for an interview _____ being ready to answer questions, but also being ready to ask them.

    a. consists of not   b. involves not only   c. is composed

3 Complete the sentences about education and jobs. Write sentences that are true for you.

1. The jobs I am most interested in fall into several categories, including *art, fashion, and theater*.

2. The educational institutions I have attended so far include _____ .

3. In my opinion, there are _____ kinds of employees in most workplaces:

   _____ .

4. For me, a good job involves _____ .

5. As an employee, I have many skills. These are _____

   _____ .

6. My job skills can be divided into several categories, including _____

   _____ .

Avoid Common Mistakes

1 Circle the mistakes.

1. An interviewer's opinion **can frequently be** (**based in**) an applicant's personal

   (a)   (b)

   appearance, **so** first impressions are important.

   (c)

2. During interviews, candidates **will be frequently** **asked** why they are **interested in**

   (a)   (b)   (c)

   the position.

3. You **might be asked** to give an example of a time when you **were involved** **on** a

   (a)   (b)   (c)

   difficult or challenging situation.

4. To ensure fairness, the same questions **that are given** to the first candidate

   (a)

   must be always given to each subsequent candidate involved **in** the interview process.

   (b)   (c)

5. If a company believes that candidates **always should** **be evaluated** by several people, a

   (a)   (b)

   team interview **will probably be used**.

   (c)

6. In some situations, people who **will later be** **supervised by** the applicant are

   (a)   (b)

   involved for his or her interview.

   (c)

7. Job applicants may not **be told** what factors a hiring decision is **based** **in**.

   (a)   (b)   (c)

8. If you **have never been** interviewed by a group of people, the experience

   (a)

   can be challenging the first time **you are involved by** it.

   (b)   (c)

2 Identify the common mistakes in the sentences. Label each sentence with the type of mistake from the box. If there is no mistake, write *d*. Then correct each sentence.

> a. Remember to place the adverb after the modal in passive sentences.
> b. Remember to use the correct preposition in the phrase *based on*.
> c. Remember to use the correct preposition in *involved in*.
> d. There is no mistake.

d One common type of question that is asked in interviews, both structured and
(1)

unstructured, is about strengths and weaknesses. _____ Applicants often may be asked to
(2)

talk about what they think their strong points and weak points are, based on the position

they are applying for. _____ It's a good idea to give some thought to this question if you are
(3)

going to be involved on a job interview. _____ When you are asked about your strengths,
(4)

try to talk about the skills you have, based in your experience. _____ You always should
(5)

be careful not to sound too proud, but if you have good skills, you should mention them.

_____ In some cultures it's considered impolite to say good things about yourself, but the
(6)

interviewer will be expecting you to do so. _____ One idea is to talk about any special
(7)

projects you have been involved. _____ You may be asked to talk about your weaknesses; in
(8)

this case, be honest but not negative. _____ The best answer may be one that is based as a
(9)

positive; for example, "I sometimes spend too much time on a project because I am trying

to do a good job."

Self-Assessment

Circle the word or phrase that correctly completes each sentence.

1. A good practice interview simulates the conditions that _____ in a real interview.

   a. will experience   b. experienced   c. will be experienced

2. At a conventional job interview, you can expect _____ about your employment
   history.

   a. to be asked   b. to ask   c. asked

3. Are interviewers _____ questions about your physical condition in an interview?

   a. allow to include   b. including   c. allowed to include

4. During the interview yesterday, Tomas _____ about his professional goals.

   a. was asked   b. has been asked   c. had been asked

5. Michelle knew that she _____ to write a piece of computer code during her interview for a programming position.

   a. might expect   b. might be expected   c. expected

6. Cristina has been _____ serve on an interview panel for a new position in her department.

   a. asked to   b. asked   c. asking

7. What do you think the manager's decision was _____?

   a. based on   b. suggested   c. based

8. In my opinion, this is a good company to work for, _____ other places I have worked.

   a. compared   b. compare   c. compared to

9. Which of these _____ of interviews have you participated in?

   a. topics   b. types   c. several

10. Depending on _____ conducting an interview, it can be one-on-one or a panel interview format.

    a. the classification of   b. the basis of   c. the number of people

11. Interviews are often _____ answering questions and demonstrating knowledge or skills.

    a. involving   b. a combination of   c. composed

12. There are a number of different ways to find a job, _____ looking online, researching the field, and talking to friends and acquaintances.

    a. including   b. consist of   c. involves

13. It has _____ that successful job applicants use a variety of strategies, and persist even when the search is discouraging.

    a. often observed   b. been often observed   c. often been observed

14. Applicants for job interviews are selected _____ to their skills and experience.

    a. according   b. depending   c. involving

15. Interviewers may use a number of techniques, _____ tests and presentations.

    a. which   b. which include   c. which are included

Classification and Definition 2
Your Ideal Job

The Language of Definition

1 Read the paragraphs about personality types. Then label the words in bold in each sentence.

> GN = general noun   DD = defining details   T = term

T (1) **Personality types** are a way of dividing people into groups to better understand them. For example, an individual may be a *people person*. This is someone

DD (2) **who enjoys the company of other people** and is very social. People in this group are also called

GN (3) **extroverts**; they usually prefer to work and relax with others. The opposite personality type is called an

GN (4) **introvert**. An introvert is a person *DD* (5) **who generally prefers to work alone**.

Holland's Hexagon Model is one example of a

DD (6) **personality type system**. This is a *GN* (7) **system** which divides people into six broad categories. Among the best-known personality systems is the Myers-Briggs Type Indicator, which divides people into 16 personality types.

Many people are curious about their personality type. One kind of personality assessment tool is a quiz. A *T* (8) **quiz** that gives the test taker his or her score immediately is a self-scoring quiz. These are easy to take and readily available online.

2 Complete the sentences about the workplace. Circle the phrase that correctly completes each sentence.

1. The skills and knowledge that allow a person to do a task or job _____ *know-how*.

   (a.) is referred to as   b. refers as   c. is referred to

2. According to the U.S. Department of Labor, employment know-how _____ competencies and foundation skills.

   a. are combinations of   √ b. is a combination of   c. that is a combination of

3. _____ effective workers can do.

   √ a. Competencies are   b. Competencies are   c. Competencies
      things that   things who   means

4. One workplace competency is the ability to use resources effectively; for example, an effective worker is one who uses _____ well.

   √ a. its time   b. their time   c. his or her time

5. Another important competency is using interpersonal skills; these _____ working well with others.

   a. are a skill that involves   b. is a skill that involves   √ c. are skills that involve

6. An employee with good interpersonal skills can work well even with co-workers who are not from _____ .

   √ a. his or her culture   b. their culture   c. his culture

7. The ability to use technology and tools appropriately _____ .

   a. are called technology   √ b. is known as technology   c. technology
      competencies   competency   competency

8. An effective worker needs to be able to work with systems. _____ understanding, designing, and improving systems, and being able to monitor and improve performance.

   a. These are defined as   √ b. This skill is defined as   c. Defined as

9. _____ the ability to get and evaluate data; to organize, interpret, and communicate information.

   √ a. An information   b. Information   c. Information
      competency   competency is   competency
      defines as

3 Unscramble the sentences about stereotypes.

1. a fixed idea / is defined as / about a group of people / a stereotype

   A stereotype is defined as a fixed idea about a group of people.

2. a stereotypical member of the group / fits this idea / a person who / is sometimes referred to as

   _____

3. as a stereotypical extrovert / might be referred to / for example, a person who / loves being with others and hates being alone

   _____

4. is called / putting people into groups / based on these ideas / stereotyping

   _____

5. treating people less well / discrimination / because they are members of a particular group / is known as

   _____

6. of discrimination / a type / stereotyping / can be defined as

   _____

7. as treating people differently / is defined / gender discrimination / depending on whether they are male or female

   _____

8. their age is called / making judgments or decisions / about people based on / age discrimination

   _____

4 Complete the sentences about John Holland's system (See pp. 172 of your Student's Book for more information.). Use the passive.

1. We call a shape that represents an idea, like John Holland's hexagonal shape, a model.

   A shape that represents an idea , like John Holland's hexagonal shape,

   is called a model .

2. In Holland's system, he refers to the six personality types, as artistic, investigative, realistic, social, enterprising, and conventional.

   In Holland's system, the six .... is refered as artistic, investigative, realistic, social, enterprising, and conventional.

3. In Holland's theory, he calls people who like to solve problems, investigative personality types.

   In Holland's theory, _____ is called investigative personality types.

4. It defines people with skills in working with records and numbers as having a conventional personality type.

People with skills in working with records and numbers

_____is defined as_____ having a conventional personality type.

5. People refer to people (or things) that get along well or work well together as compatible.

People (or things) that get along well or work well together

_____is refered to as_____ .

6. We would define incompatible people as people who do not get along well.

_Incompatible People is defined as_____ people who do not get along well.

7. In Holland's theoretical model, we refer to the two environments closest to each personality type as compatible environments.

In Holland's theoretical model, the two environments closest to each personality type

_____is refered to as_____ compatible environments.

8. When ideas about human behavior seem likely but would be difficult to prove, people often call them theories.

When ideas about human behavior seem likely but would be difficult to prove,

_____is offten called theories_____ .

Appositives

1 Complete the sentences about personality types. Circle the phrase that best completes each sentence.

1. Personality instruments, _____ , can help you choose a satisfying job or field of study.

   a. are assessments used to show an individual's preferences or personality type

   (b.) assessments used to show an individual's preferences or personality type

   c. assessments show an individual's preferences or personality type

2. One well-known personality instrument is the Keirsey Temperament Sorter, _____ .

   (a.) theories developed by David Keirsey

   b. theory developed by David Keirsey

   c. a theory developed by David Keirsey

3. This instrument is designed to give insight into a person's _____ .

   √a. temperament (the aspects of our personality that determine moods and behavior)

   b. temperament, (the aspects of our personality that determine moods and behavior)

   c. temperament the aspects of our personality that determine moods and behavior

4. Another popular instrument is the _____ .

   a. Myers-Briggs Type Indicator, (MBTI)

   √b. Myers-Briggs Type Indicator (MBTI)

   c. Myers-Briggs Type Indicator, (MBTI),

5. Both the Keirsey Temperament Sorter and the Myers-Briggs Type Indicator are based on the work of Carl Jung, _____ .

   √a. a Swiss psychiatrist who lived from 1875 to 1961

   b. a way of dividing people into personality groups

   c. two psychiatrists from Switzerland

6. These instruments are similar in that they measure preferences – _____ – not skills.

   a. what we are very good at

   b. what we prefer to measure

   √c. what we prefer to do when we have a choice

7. Both instruments categorize people according to the way they process information and interact with their social environment (_____).

   √a. which is the information around them

   b. meaning the air, water, and land

   c. the world they live or work in

8. Personality types should never be seen as good or bad; each type has the same potential – _____ – as every other type.

   a. the ability to develop and succeed

   b. a type of potential

   √ c. a better type of personality

9. For example, kinesthetic learners _____ can learn things just as well as any other learner.

   a. , people who learn best through movement

   b. who are people who learn best through movement –

   √ c. , people who learn best through movement,

2 Match the phrases to correctly complete each sentence.

1. The idea of different types of personalities, a popular theory in the study of psychology, _d_ .

2. Among my co-workers, _b_ , there are several different personality types.

3. Kelly, our office manager, _f_ .

4. Rodrigo, _i_ , likes working with numbers and is an expert with budgets.

5. Jin Sun is a perfect illustration of a social personality type, _h_ , so she is a great receptionist.

6. Isabel hates writing monthly reports; people with her personality type – _e_ – don't like structured activities or tasks.

7. I guess I'm the investigative type. I enjoy solving problems (_____).

8. Our work requires a lot of collaboration (_g_) and dedication.

9. I think that our compatibility (our ability to get along and work well together) _a_ .

9 - a. a group of people who have worked together for years

2 - b. is due to our understanding each others' personality types

7 - c. something I find myself having to do frequently

d. comes alive in many workplace situations

6 - e. artistic and creative people

3 - f. is really well organized and can find anything you need

8 - g. working together on projects

5 - h. a person who is good at working with people

4 - i. our accountant and data manager

3 Rewrite the sentences about Tina. Use an appositive for the words in bold. Also use the punctuation in parentheses.

1. Tina is **my cousin** and she is very good at helping people. (commas)

   Tina, my cousin, is very good at helping people.

2. She's a good example of a social personality type; that is (**a personality type that enjoys working with others**.) (parentheses)

   _____

   _____

3. Tina does human resources work; this is **work helping other employees and job applicants**. (parentheses)

   _____

4. Tina works in the Employee Relations Support Office; they call it **ERSO**. (parentheses)   .(ERSO)

   _____

5. Her job is full-time; it's **40 hours a week**. (parentheses)

   _____

6. She's a Human Resources Specialist; that is **a mid-level position**. (comma)

   She, a Human Resources Specialist, is a mid-level Position

7. At her company, a personality assessment is given to all new employees; it's called **the Workplace Compatibility Inventory**. (commas)   ⁹ is called

   _____

8. Tina says that the WCI is **a test researched and designed by her company** and that it helps people work together. (dashes)

   _____

4 Complete the sentences using appositives. Write sentences that are true for you.

1. <u>Rice</u> , one of the most popular foods in my country, is <u>both delicious and nutritious</u> .

2. The president of the United States, _____ , is

_____ .

3. I like going to _____ , a great place for

_____ , because _____ .

4. My professor, a person who _____ ,

_____ .

5. My closest friend, _____ , is

_____ .

6. My home country, _____ , produces

_____ , and _____ .

Avoid Common Mistakes

1 Circle the mistakes.

1. What **personal characteristics** are **defined** as (the one) that good leaders should have?

(a)   (b)   (c)

2. Two skills **that leaders should have** are the ability to lead people and the ability to lead

(a)

change. **They** need to have **both of** them.

(b)   (c)

3. Leading people **are define** as being able to guide **others** to work effectively to meet the

(a)   (b)

goals **that** the organization has established.

(c)

4. Leading people **includes** managing any disagreements or difficult interpersonal

(a)

situations **who** may come up; this **is called** conflict management.

(b)   (c)

5. Thought leaders **are a person who** influence the way others view an issue.

(a) (b) (c)

6. People who **are** good at leading change **use** creativity and innovation to motivate

(a)   (b)

employees; they encourage others to use **them**, too.

(c)

7. Another important skill, leveraging diversity, **defines** as leading a workplace where

(a)

individual differences **are valued**.

(b)   (c)

8. A leader **which** does not have **these** skills will not be as successful as one who **does**.

(a)   (b)   (c)

2 Identify the common mistakes in the sentences. Label each sentence with the type of mistake from the box. If there is no mistake, write *e*. Then correct each sentence.

a. Remember to use singular and plural nouns correctly in definitions.

b. Remember to use the correct verb form in the passive when giving definitions.

c. Remember to use the correct pronoun in relative clauses. Specifically, remember to use *who* only with animate nouns.

d. Be sure that pronoun use is clear.

e. There is no mistake.

<u>*a*</u> Effective leadership is ~~skills~~ *a skill* that is important not only in the workplace, but in
(1)

the community as well. ____ Leading people and leading change are two skills who
(2)

leaders need to have. ____ They are not the only ones. ____ Effective leaders need to
(3)   (4)

be accountable, or willing to hold themselves responsible for both good work and for

mistakes. ____ They need to be what are referred to as "politically savvy"; that is, able
(5)

to act appropriately according to the internal and external politics at work in the

organization. ____ A leader which is not able to do this is likely to run into difficulties.
(6)

____ Leaders need business acumen, which is defining as the ability to manage human,
(7)

money, and information resources well. ____ Without them, it is difficult to manage an
(8)

organization. ____ Finally, a good leader needs to be results driven; this means that he
(9)

or she is people who meet goals and expectations. ____ A person who has all of these
(10)

skills is likely to be effective at what he or she does, and a good leader.

Self-Assessment

Circle the word or phrase that correctly completes each sentence.

1. Psychologists are _____ study human behavior.

   a. specialists   b. who   c. specialists who

2. A personality type assessment is an instrument that helps individuals find _____ personality type.

   a. his   b. her   c. their

3. Linguistic, logical/mathematical, and musical/rhythmic are three _____ intelligences.

   a. types of   b. types   c. type of

4. Spatial intelligence is _____ the ability to understand space and the relationships between things in space.

   a. called   b. defined as   c. referred to

5. Howard Gardner, a psychologist and _____ the author of the theory of multiple intelligences.

   a. researcher, is   b. researcher is   c. researcher, he is

6. Gardner's approach _____ identifies nine different intelligences.

   a. , a psychological   b. , a psychological   c. a psychological
      breakthrough   breakthrough,   breakthrough

7. In Gardner's system, interpersonal intelligence _____ the ability to understand other people.

   a. defined   b. is defined   c. is defined as

8. The ability to use language to express yourself and to understand others is _____ linguistic intelligence.

   a. called   b. referred to   c. defined as

9. A self-aware person is one who has a realistic picture and opinion of _____ abilities and personality.

   a. the   b. his or her   c. their

10. Employees in an organization's workforce are sometimes _____ to as its *human capital*.

    a. called   b. referred   c. defined

11. The feeling that the work one does is worthwhile and rewarding _____ job satisfaction.

    a. is known as   b. known as   c. knows as

12. Finding a career that fits with your _____ is likely to increase your job satisfaction.

    a. type (personality   b. type personality   c. type, (personality
       or intelligence)   or intelligence   or intelligence)

13. Talking with a career counselor _____ individual who is trained to help you identify possible careers, is always a good idea.

    a. and   b. , an   c. an

14. People who are self-possessed generally don't display _____ emotions in public.

    a. his   b. his or her   c. their

15. An auditory learner is someone who uses _____ sense of hearing to absorb and process information.

    a. its   b. his or her   c. their

Problem–Solution 1

Food and Technology

Present Perfect and Present Perfect Progressive

1 Unscramble the sentences about genetically modified (GM) foods.

1. product / eaten / modified / you / genetically / a / have / ever

   Have you ever eaten a genetically modified product?

2. already / GM / most / foods / eaten / have / people

   People have already eaten most GM foods.

3. a / seen / label / you / supermarket / ever / have / a / GM / in

   Have you ever seen a GM label in a supermarket?

4. labels / have / in / these / never / most / supermarkets / people / seen

   People have never seen these lables in most supermarkets.

5. never / GM / been / many / have / ingredients / able / to / consumers / identify

   Many ingredients have never been able to consumers GM identify

6. have / supermarkets / many / foods / labeled / not / GM / yet

   Many supermarkets have not labeled GM foods yet.

7. has / the / labels / already / GM / government / proposed / food

   The government has already proposed

8. this / law / yet / become / not / has / however,

   However, this has not become law yet.

2 Complete the sentences about salmon production. Use the <u>simple present</u>, <u>simple past</u>, <u>present perfect progressive</u>, or <u>present perfect</u> form of the verbs in parentheses. Sometimes more than one answer is possible.

The Food and Drug Administration (FDA) <u>*has received/received*</u> (receive) many
                                                          (1)

applications for permission to genetically alter Atlantic salmon in recent weeks.

Decisions will be made in the coming months. In response to this, the FDA

<u>has arranged</u> (arrange) a public meeting to discuss the issues. In preparation for the
      (2)

meeting, the FDA <u>has released</u> (release) information on its website about the history
                        (3)

of salmon production. Here is an excerpt:

Atlantic salmon <u>has</u> always
                          (4)

<u>been</u> (be) overfished, and this trend
      (4)

<u>continues</u> (continue) today. Because of
      (5)

its health benefits, fish consumption

<u>has increased</u> (increase) dramatically in the
      (6)

last 10 years. In recent years, the Atlantic salmon

population <u>has decreased</u> (decrease) partly
                  (7)

because of this. In fact, the Atlantic salmon <u>becomes</u> (become) endangered in
                                                      has (8)ecome

many parts of New England today.

Fish farming <u>provide</u> (provide) one answer to the problem of overfishing.
                    (9)

The farming of salmon <u>started</u> (start) in Norway in the 1960s. Since then, fish
                              (10)

farms <u>has becomes</u> (become) one of the main sources of fish around the world. They
        (11)

<u>has</u> (be) very successful, despite the fact that there <u>has</u> (be)
      (12)   (13)

a great deal of controversy over this practice in recent years.

3 Read the web article about genetically modified animals. Circle the verb form that correctly completes each sentence.

In recent years, there **(has been)** / **is** a great deal of
(1)
interest in genetically modified animals. More and more

people **were concerned** / **(have been concerned)**
(2)
about the potential dangers of GM animals. On

Monday, the Food and Drug Administration (FDA)

has released / **(released)** a report on genetically
(3)
modified animals. The report reveals some surprising information about GM animals,

and many consumers and animal rights activists were shocked by the report.

According to the FDA, the genetic modification of animals **(has not been)** / **is not**
(4)
a new practice. People **(have been using)** / **used** GM technologies to enhance food
(5)
products since agriculture was invented thousands of years ago. Currently, scientists

(have used) / **are using** this technology to enhance the production of animals for food.
(6)
The report **is** / **(has been)** the subject of criticism since it was released on Monday.
(7)
Critics say that only the beneficial aspects of GM animals have been included. An

FDA spokesperson **(denied)** / **has been denying** this claim yesterday, saying that the
(8)
FDA received input from groups such as animal rights activists and consumers.

4 A Read the sentences about Dr. Boris Ivanov, a researcher. Write the present perfect or present perfect progressive form of the verb in parentheses. Sometimes more than one answer is possible.

Meat from genetically modified animals _has been_ (be) available for the past few years.
(1)

Recently, however, scientists _____ (work) on a way to create meat in a
(2)

laboratory. Scientists _____ (grow) cells in laboratories since 1907. For the
(3)

last 20 years, they _____ (use) this technology for medical applications.
(4)

One researcher, Dr. Boris Ivanov at the Bay City Institute, _____ (employ)
(5)

this technology to create meat in a laboratory for human consumption. He

_____ (take) cells from a chicken and adding to them a chemical that
(6)

promotes growth. His work _____ (result) in an edible meat product.
(7)

Laboratory meat _____ (receive) a great deal of attention in the news
(8)

media. Animal rights activists _____ (be) interested in the future of
(9)

laboratory-generated meat. Some organizations _____ (offer) grants to
(10)

scientists who work in this area.

B Read the sentences in A again. Then answer the question.

Which sentences in A have more than one correct answer? _____

5 Rewrite the sentences. Use the present perfect passive to represent the words in bold.

1. **Companies have listed** ingredients on food packages since 1913.

   Ingredients _have been listed_ on food packages since 1913.

2. **The government has not required** GM food labeling yet.

   GM food labeling _____ yet.

3. **Companies have used** GM ingredients in many popular snack foods.

   GM ingredients _____ in many popular snack foods.

4. **Researchers have conducted** a number of studies on consumer awareness of GM ingredients.

A number of studies _____ on consumer awareness of GM ingredients.

5. **Researchers have collected** statistics on consumers' attitudes toward the use of GM ingredients.

Statistics _____ on consumers' attitudes toward the use of GM ingredients.

6. **Researchers have asked** a number of people if they thought foods with GM ingredients were safe.

A number of people _____ if they thought foods with GM ingredients were safe.

7. **Researchers have also polled** people on the benefits of labeling foods with GM ingredients.

People _____ on the benefits of labeling foods with GM ingredients.

8. **Researchers have invited** supermarket chains and food service professionals to participate in these polls as well.

Supermarket chains and food service professionals _____ to participate in these polls as well.

Common Noun Phrase Structures

1 Circle the noun phrase that correctly completes each sentence.

1. _____ *locavorism* is restricting food choices to locally produced items.

   (a.) The definition of   b. The number of   c. The effects of

2. Sustainability is _____ locavorism because it has positive effects on the environment.

   a. the rest of   b. the number of   c. the heart of

3. _____ consuming only locally produced food is to reduce the distances that food travels from farms to consumers' tables, called "food miles."

   a. The definition of   b. The purpose of   c. The amount of

4. _____ reducing food miles is to reduce our ecological footprint.

   a. The purpose of   b. The majority of   c. The number of

5. _____ reducing food miles include limiting the use of fossil fuels and bringing fresher products to consumers.

    a. The effect of   b. The number of   c. The effects of

6. _____ eating locally is gradually becoming more popular.

    a. The notion of   b. The definition of   c. The rest of

7. _____ supermarket chains have begun labeling items as "locally grown."

    a. The number of   b. The effects of   c. A number of

8. _____ labeling produce as "locally grown" is often an increase in sales.

    a. The result of   b. The majority of   c. The basis of

2 Read the paragraph about food labeling. Choose a noun phrase from the box to complete each sentence. Sometimes more than one answer is possible, and you may use some noun phrases more than once.

a number of	the importance of	the number of	the results of	the essence of
the goal of	the majority of	the purpose of	the definition of	

A poll on food labeling was recently conducted. _The purpose of/The goal of_ the (1) poll was to determine the public's awareness of the term *natural* when applied to food products. Specifically, _____ (2) the survey was to discover the extent to which consumers understand the meaning of this term. _____ (3) the survey showed that _____ (4) the people questioned did not understand the precise meaning of *natural*. _____ (5) the poll therefore indicate that consumer education is lacking in this area. _____ (6) understanding the meaning of this term is clear when one is making choices at the supermarket. For example, consumers need to be aware of _____ (7) varying conditions that the term *natural* may describe. This is an issue because _____ (8) products labeled "natural" may in fact contain ingredients derived from natural sources, but these ingredients may have undergone processing.

_____ (9) respondents in this study who equated *natural* with concepts such as "organic" or "healthy" was surprisingly high. _____ (10) the term *natural* can be understood in many ways, as can the term *organic*. _____ (11) these ideas implies healthy, unprocessed foods. However, consumers must be informed about where their produce comes from before trusting anything with an *organic* label.

3 Complete the sentences about organic produce. Write noun phrases with *that* using the words in parentheses in the correct blank.

1. _____ I am concerned about *the fact that*
   (a)   (b)
   pesticides have been proven to be harmful. (fact)

2. _____ U.S. government agencies promote
   (a)
   _____ there is no nutritional difference
   (b)
   between organic produce and conventionally grown
   produce. (notion)

3. _____ I disagree with _____
   (a)   (b)
   organic produce is healthier than conventionally grown
   produce. (assumption)

4. Many people are not aware of _____
   (a)
   some produce labeled "organic" is actually grown on
   _____ farms that use pesticides. (fact)
   (b)

5. Many consumers base their choices on _____ organic farming is less harmful
   (a)
   to the environment than _____ conventional farming practices. (idea)
   (b)

6. In most countries, _____ organic produce is more expensive than
   (a)
   conventionally grown produce makes it _____ unattractive for people on a
   (b)
   budget. (belief)

7. A major obstacle has been _____ organic produce is simply unavailable in
   (a)
   _____ some communities. (fact)
   (b)

8. Now more than ever, _____ people of all income levels must have access to
   (a)
   fresh produce has inspired _____ community organizers to bring farmers'
   (b)
   markets to inner city neighborhoods. (view)

4 Write sentences about three of the topics in the list using the noun phrases in the box.

the concept of	the fact that	the importance of	the purpose of
the effects of	the idea of/that	the potential consequences of	the possibility that

Topics

genetically modified animals   labeling GM food   locally produced food

genetically modified produce   laboratory-created meat   organic produce

1. *The concept of meat created in a lab is very unappealing. The possibility that consumers would buy it is ridiculous.*

2. _____

_____

3. _____

_____

4. _____

_____

Avoid Common Mistakes

1 Circle the mistakes.

1. **A** number of (**expert agrees**) that we should **label** GM ingredients.
   (a)   (b)   (c)

2. Recent **researches** **shows** that organic food **has** health benefits.
          (a)   (b)   (c)

3. **This** fact that we do not know the **effects** of GM food indicates that more **research**
    (a)   (b)   (c)
   needs to be done.

4. **Most** consumers were not aware of **this** fact that supermarkets sell **many** foods with
    (a)   (b)   (c)
   GM ingredients.

5. A number of **scientist agrees** that industrial food production **methods** **are** harmful to
               (a)   (b)   (c)
   the environment.

6. There is a great **deal** of **informations** on the environmental effects of meat **production**.
            (a)   (b)   (c)

7. A number of **expert believes** that we should **find** **alternatives** to pesticides.
               (a)   (b)   (c)

8. A major obstacle is **this** fact that organic **produce** is more expensive than produce
               (a)   (b)
   grown with **pesticides**.
         (c)

2 Identify the common mistakes in the sentences. Label each sentence with the type of mistake from the box. If there is no mistake, write *d*. Then correct each sentence.

a. Remember that noncount nouns such as *advice*, *equipment*, *research*, *information*, *knowledge*, and *evidence* do not have plural forms.
b. Remember to use *the fact that*, and not *this fact that*.
c. Remember that *a number of* takes a plural count noun and plural verb.
d. There is no mistake.

               experts point

<u>c</u> A number of ~~expert points~~ to the benefits of eating and growing organic produce.
(1)

_____ Organic produce is produce grown without the use of pesticides. _____ There is a great
(2)   (3)

deal of informations on the negative effects of pesticides. _____ A number of scientist agree
(4)

with the fact that pesticides cause a variety of health problems in humans. _____ For example,
(5)

researches show that pesticides can cause damage to the nervous and reproductive systems

of humans. _____ A number of study shows that when children are given a diet of organic
(6)

produce, pesticide levels in their bodies drop dramatically. _____ In addition, most experts
(7)

agree with this fact that the use of pesticides is unsustainable. _____ This is because pesticides
(8)

affect the soil, as well as insects and other living creatures. _____ This fact that pesticides build
(9)

up in the soil and remain there for many years means that the soil is less able to support plant

life as time goes on. _____ There is a great deal of evidences that organic farming practices
(10)

reverse the process of soil damage, essentially keeping it clean and healthy for generations

to come.

Self-Assessment

Circle the word or phrase that correctly completes each sentence.

1. Many people have not _____ a GM label in the supermarket.

   a. saw   b. seen   c. see

2. GM foods have _____ in some countries in Europe.

   a. not been accepted   b. not accepted   c. not been accepting

3. In 2011, the Great Foods Company _____ not to sell any GM products.

   a. decided   b. has decided   c. has been deciding

4. Recently, there _____ a great deal of concern about food safety.

   a. is   b. has been   c. had

5. The FDA _____ a number of applications to genetically modify animals in recent months.

   a. receives   b. has been receiving   c. has been received

6. People have been creating meat in laboratories _____ .

   a. for several years now   b. in 2005   c. in months

7. GM ingredients _____ in a number of snack foods.

   a. have been using   b. have used   c. have been used

8. _____ consumer education is better health.

   a. The rest of   b. The goal of   c. The number of

9. _____ of *genetic engineering* is making changes to the genes of a plant or an animal.

   a. The importance   b. The fact   c. The definition

10. Consumer awareness is _____ the FDA's report on GM foods.

    a. the purpose of   b. the amount of   c. the definition of

11. The researcher, Dr. Smith, cites _____ the genetic modification of animals is not new.

    a. the amount of   b. the number of   c. the fact that

12. Some people disagree with _____ GM foods are safe.

    a. the idea the   b. the idea that   c. the idea of

13. A number of _____ that eating organic produce has health benefits.

    a. study shows   b. study show   c. studies show

14. There is a great deal of _____ on the effects of pesticides on humans.

    a. informations   b. information   c. the information

15. Few people are aware of _____ the use of GM ingredients has increased dramatically in recent years.

    a. this fact that   b. a fact that   c. the fact that

Problem–Solution 2
Children and Health

Reporting Verbs

1 A Complete the sentences about children and exercise. Use the present form of the words in the box. Sometimes more than one answer is possible.

| believe | describe | emphasize | show | recommend | suggest |

1. The pamphlet _describes_ six strategies for improving the health and well-being of Bay City's children.

2. The city council _____ several low-cost ways to encourage children to get more exercise.

3. Community organizers _____ that building a skateboarding park in the city will encourage children to be more active.

4. The traffic committee _____ adding more bicycle lanes so children will be able to ride their bikes to school.

5. The committee further _____ offering free bike safety courses.

6. The report _____ the low cost of many of these proposals.

7. Experts _____ that these measures will affect the psychological health of the city's children, as well as their physical health.

8. Chart 1 _____ the projected cost of the projects.

9. Illustration 5 _____ that the cost will come from taxes.

10. Mayor Green said, "I _____ these proposals will benefit the entire community."

11. He _____ that the city should start these projects as soon as possible.

12. Mayor Green _____ that the city will become a more desirable and healthier place in which to live.

B Read the sentences in A again. Then answer the question.

In which sentence in A can you add *that*? _____

2 Complete the sentences about childhood obesity. Circle the reporting verbs that best express the meanings given.

1. neutral in tone; reporting a fact

   The CDC (2009) (reports)/ claims that 60 percent of school-aged children consume at least one can of soda every day.

2. likely, but still uncertain

   Wu (2010) **predicts / suggests** that children who consume sugary drinks have a greater chance of becoming obese.

3. opinion

   However, Johnson (2010) **believes / shows** that there is no evidence that consuming sugar leads to obesity.

4. likely, but still uncertain

   Moreno's data (2011) **investigates / suggests** that reducing sugar intake reduces blood sugar levels.

5. you are unsure that this is true

   The CDC **illustrated / alleged** that 70 percent of obese youth had at least one risk factor for cardiovascular disease.

6. opinion

   A CDC study **reports / suggests** that obese children are at greater risk for psychological problems.

7. results

   Brown's study (2011) **suggests / demonstrates** that obese adolescents get lower scores on self-esteem assessment tests.

8. you are unsure that this is true

   A 2009 report **claims / shows** that the relationship between obesity and self-esteem is cultural.

9. results

   Smith (2010) **concluded / recommended** that there is no connection between obesity and self-esteem in certain cultures.

10. likely, but still uncertain

    Washington (2011) **proposes / states** that weight affects the self-esteem of girls more than boys.

3 A researcher, Ingrid Rosen, published a study on obesity in 2011. Write her opinions. Use the reporting verbs in parentheses.

1. Obesity is a cultural issue. (believe)

   Rosen believes that obesity is a cultural issue.

2. There is not necessarily a relationship between obesity and self-esteem. (argue)

   _____

3. Not all adolescents who are overweight have psychological problems. (show)

   _____

4. Certain cultures do not consider obesity unattractive. (emphasize)

   _____

5. Certain cultures do not consider obesity unhealthy. (recognize)

   _____

Adverb Clauses and Phrases with As

1 Complete the sentences about accident rates for young workers. Circle the verb that best completes the *as* phrase.

1. As **seen** / **shows** in Table 7, three factors affect the young worker accident rate.

2. As **can see** / **can be seen** in Table 8, the number of hours worked affects the youth accident rate.

3. As Chart 4 **demonstrates** / **can be demonstrated**, time of day has an effect on the youth accident rate.

4. As **shown** / **shows** in Chart 2, job training for young workers reduces the injury rate by 33 percent.

5. As **demonstrated** / **can demonstrate** by Figure 3, a higher percentage of accidents among young people occur after six working hours.

6. As Chart 4 **shown** / **shows**, young people who leave work by 6:00 p.m. have lower accident rates.

7. As Chart 2 **points out** / **shown**, accident rates increase after 6:00 p.m.

8. As **illustrates** / **illustrated** in Figure 3, young workers are 56 percent more likely to have an accident between the hours of 9 p.m. and midnight.

9. As Chart 2 **can be seen** / **points out**, an increase in the number of job training hours that young workers receive greatly reduces the chances of on-the-job accidents.

2 Look at the chart. Complete the sentences with an *as* phrase. Use the active (A) or passive (P) form of the verbs in parentheses.

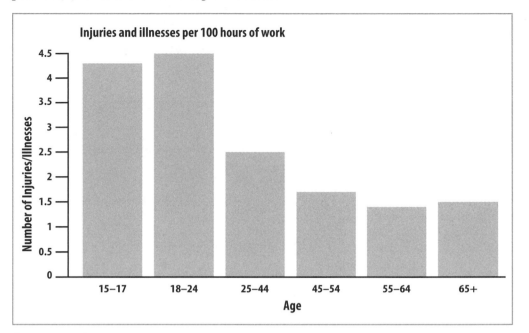

Source: www.cdc.gov

1. _As the chart demonstrates_ , workers aged 18–24 have the highest rate of work-related injuries and illnesses. (demonstrate, A)

2. _____ , the rates of work-related injuries and illnesses go down after age 24. (show, P)

3. _____ , young workers have more work-related injuries and illnesses than older workers. (see, P)

4. _____ , workers aged 55–64 have the lowest rate of work-related injuries and illnesses. (show, A)

5. _____ , workers 65 and older have only 1.5 injuries and illnesses per 100 hours of work. (demonstrate, P)

6. _____ , workers aged 18–24 have 4.5 injuries and illnesses per 100 hours of work. (illustrate, A)

7. _____ , adolescent workers are more likely to suffer from work-related injuries than workers in their 30s and 40s. (illustrate, P)

8. _____ , workers aged 15–17 have a rate of 4.3 injuries and illnesses per 100 hours of work. (point out, A)

Common Vocabulary for Describing Information in Graphics

1 Look at the bar graph. Circle the word or phrase that correctly completes each sentence.

1. The bar graph **shows that** / **shows** the percentage of students participating in physical activity by gender and by age.

2. The graph shows that the amount of exercise boys and girls get **declines** / **increases** with age.

3. From the graph, it **shows** / **can be** concluded that girls between the ages of 14–18 get less exercise than girls between the ages of 9–13.

4. From the graph, it can be concluded that there is a **rise** / **decline** in participation in physical education over time.

5. From the graph, it can be seen that there is a **slight** / **sharp** decline in participation in family activities among adolescent girls.

6. From the graph, it can be inferred that there is a **fluctuation** / **drop** in the desire to exercise as children age.

7. There is a **dramatic** / **slow** decrease in the amount of participation in physical education between girls 9–13 and girls 14–18.

8. Participation in team sports **dropped** / **rose** by about 25 percent between boys 9–13 and boys 14–18.

9. There is a **steady** / **rapid** decrease in the amount of exercise that children get as they age.

10. There is a steep **rise** / **fall** in gym use for exercise as girls age.

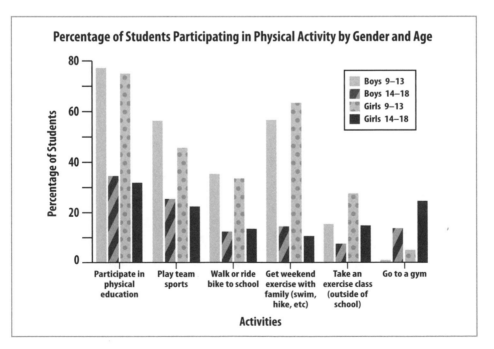

2 A Read the statements about the bar graph. Write *T* (true) or *F* (false).

1. _*F*_ The percentage of girls who go to a gym for exercise declines as they age.

2. _____ Participation in family activities decreases as girls age.

3. _____ There is a slight decrease between the percent of boys 9–13 and the percent of boys 14–18 who walk to school.

4. _____ There is a sudden increase in participation in family exercise as boys age.

5. _____ Participation in team sports decreases by about 23 percent as girls age.

B Write sentences about the statements in A. Use these reporting phrases: *The graph* + verb (active), *From the graph*, *it* + verb (passive).

1. _The graph shows that the percentage of girls who go to a gym for exercise_
   increases as they age.

2. _____

3. _____

4. _____

5. _____

6. _____

Avoid Common Mistakes

1 Circle the mistakes.

1. As (the) Chart 1 **shows**, activity rates **declined** over time.
   (a)   (b)   (c)

2. From **this** study, it **can seen** **that** high school children are less active than elementary
   (a)   (b)   (c)
   school children.

3. **Table** C **shows** **that** improved health in cities with bike lanes.
   (a)   (b)   (c)

4. From **the** table, it **can inferred** **that** active families have lower body weights.
   (a)   (b)   (c)

5. As **the** Figure 1 **shows**, teenagers who do not work **miss** fewer days of school.
   (a)   (b)   (c)

6. From **the** chart, it **can seen** **that** there is a connection between genetics and
   (a)   (b)   (c)
   body weight.

7. **Table** A **shows** **that** the results of adding two hours of PE per week at three
   (a)   (b)   (c)
   public schools.

8. As **the** Chart 2 **illustrates**, people who followed the same diet had very different **results**.
   (a)   (b)   (c)

2 Identify the common mistakes in the sentences. Label each sentence with the type of mistake from the box. If there is no mistake, write *d*. Then correct each sentence.

a. Remember to use the base form of *be* after modals in the passive.	c. In general, when referring to a chart, graph, study, or other source with *As . . .*, do not use an article.
b. Remember that reporting verbs such as *show*, *demonstrate*, and *illustrate* can be followed by a *that* clause or by a noun phrase, but not by both.	d. There is no mistake.

b A recent study shows ~~that~~ the dramatic effect that simple lifestyle changes can
(1)
have on childhood obesity and obesity-related illnesses such as high blood pressure and

Type 2 diabetes. _____ As the Lee's 2010 study shows, children who exercised just one
(2)
additional hour per week lowered their blood pressure. _____ As the Figure 1 shows, study
(3)
participants lowered their blood pressure by an average of 30 percent. _____ Another
(4)
study demonstrates that a significant drop in body weight by adding only 2 hours of

activity per week. _____ As the Figure 2 shows, 100 children lost an average of 15 pounds
(5)
in three months. _____ From this study, it can inferred that children can achieve a steady
(6)
weight loss by increasing their activity levels only slightly. _____ Finally, Green's 2011 study
(7)
shows that the case of a group of 150 children with Type 2 diabetes. _____ As the Figure
(8)
3 shows, by increasing their activity levels to 30 minutes per day, over half of the children

in the group were able to stop taking diabetes medication. _____ Clearly, the study shows
(9)
some very encouraging results. _____ From these and other studies, it can seen that small
(10)
changes can have big results.

Self-Assessment

Circle the word or phrase that correctly completes each sentence.

1. The study _____ that 52 percent of adolescents at Bay School are overweight.

   a. reported   b. recommended   c. predicted

2. The report _____ 10 factors that cause obesity in children.

   a. shows that   b. states that   c. describes

3. Smith (2011) _____ that obesity among children has increased in the past 15 years.

   a. describes   b. reports   c. investigates

4. In his very thorough and convincing study, Ruiz (2009) _____ that consuming low fat foods contributes to obesity.

   a. alleges   b. shows   c. recommends

5. Yee (2010) _____ obesity is genetic.

   a. can be shown   b. believes that   c. displays that

6. Fine (2012) _____ that obesity is caused by a virus, but no one has proven this yet.

   a. claims   b. estimates   c. demonstrates

7. The chart _____ the six major causes of obesity.

   a. shows that   b. shows   c. is shown

8. As _____ by the graph, the rates of obesity in this group are higher among boys than girls.

   a. demonstrated   b. demonstrates   c. Figure 1 demonstrates

9. As can _____ , students' physical fitness declined when PE class was reduced to three days a week.

   a. be seen in Chart A   b. shown in Chart A   c. Chart A shows

10. From the chart, it can _____ that lack of physical education has a direct connection to obesity.

    a. infer   b. be inferred   c. infers that

11. The rate of participation went from 2 percent to 42 percent over five weeks. There was a(n) _____ in the number of students who participated.

    a. fluctuation   b. drop   c. increase

12. There was a _____ in obesity among the study participants. Ninety-five percent of the students in the study lost 35 pounds or more.

    a. sharp drop   b. sharp rise   c. slight increase

13. As _____ shows, children who participate in after-school sports have lower body weights than children who do not.

    a. Table C   b. a Table C   c. the Table C

14. From this study, it _____ that not consuming sugary soft drinks results in lower body weights.

    a. can see   b. can be seen   c. seen

15. This research clearly _____ link between body weight and blood pressure.

    a. demonstrates that a   b. demonstrates   c. demonstrates a

Problem–Solution 3

Health and Technology

Adverb Clauses of Purpose and Infinitives of Purpose

1 Complete the sentences about the Healthy Lifestyle website. Write *so* or *so that* in the correct blanks. Sometimes both answers are possible. Capitalize the first word of the sentence and add commas when necessary.

1. _____ The Healthy Lifestyle website provides accurate and useful nutrition advice
   (a)
   so/so that users feel better informed about issues related to health and exercise.
   (b)

2. _____ the site educates users about food and nutrition _____ people can make
   (a)   (b)
   wise diet choices.

3. _____ users can keep track of their daily intake of calories, vitamins, and minerals
   (a)

   _____ the site includes nutrition charts on a wide variety of foods.
   (b)

4. _____ Healthy Lifestyle suggests that users get a physical exam _____ they
   (a)   (b)
   know they are healthy enough to start a diet.

5. _____ users will feel that their membership is a good deal _____ Healthy
   (a)   (b)
   Lifestyle publishes articles on a wide variety of topics.

6. _____ the site asks for personal information _____ Healthy Lifestyle doctors
   (a)   (b)
   and nutritionists can design the best weight-loss program for each individual.

7. _____ users will feel confident about the privacy of their information _____
      (a)   (b)
   Healthy Lifestyle publishes a privacy statement.

8. _____ Healthy Lifestyle provides downloadable calorie charts _____ users have
      (a)   (b)
   a reference to take to stores and restaurants.

2 Complete the sentences about the Paramount Medical Group. Use adverb clauses and
infinitives of purpose, and the correct form of the words in parentheses.

1. Medical practices use electronic communication and record-keeping processes

   in order to save time and money. (in order to; save)

2. The Paramount Medical Group answers health questions by e-mail _____

   patients come to the office unnecessarily. (so as to; not have)

3. The Paramount Medical Group sends appointment reminders by text message

   _____ so many phone calls. (in order to; not make)

4. Dr. Sands created a "Frequently Asked Questions" page for the practice's Web site

   _____ the number of phone calls he receives. (in order to; cut down on)

5. Dr. Yee sent his office staff to a seminar _____ their computer skills.

   (in order to; improve)

6. Dr. Ramirez's patients e-mail her with their symptoms before the appointment

   _____ consultation time more efficiently. (so as to; use)

7. The physician's assistant researches medications online _____ accurate and

   up-to-date prescription information to patients. (in order to; give)

8. All medical records at the Paramount Medical Group are electronic _____

   paper. (so as to; not waste)

9. The Paramount Medical Group has implemented a new record-keeping system

   _____ important patient information. (in order to; not lose)

3 A Complete the sentences about physicians. Circle the words that correctly complete each sentence.

1. What do doctors need to learn **(to)** / **so that** communicate with patients from different backgrounds?

2. As surprising as it may seem, some doctors do not understand that they need to smile **to / so that** put patients at ease.

3. **To / So that** they can better treat patients, many physicians require training in behavior that acknowledges the patient's feelings and background, called "bedside manner."

4. For example, medical schools offer courses in bedside manner **to / so that** physicians will be more sensitive to patients' needs.

5. They offer training in reading facial expressions and body language **to / so that** physicians can better interpret patients' feelings.

6. Many physicians also need to understand cultural differences in medicine and health **in order to / so that** treat patients from different cultures.

7. For example, many physicians forget not **to / so that** make eye contact with patients from certain cultures.

8. **To / So that** help with this, the Centers for Disease Control (CDC) publishes a series of pamphlets on cross-cultural communication.

9. The pamphlets include topics such as eye contact and touching in several cultures **to / so that** physicians will be aware of the cultural issues that they need to understand.

B Read the sentences in A again. Then answer the question.

Which sentences in A are examples of repetitive use of *to*? _____ On a separate piece of paper, rewrite the sentences to avoid repetition.

Reducing Adverb Clauses to Phrases

1 Rewrite the words in bold as reduced adverb clauses.

1. **When they are looking** for a new doctor, many people start their search online.

   When looking for a new doctor, many people start their search online.

2. **Before you start** to search online, read these tips.

   _____ to search online, read these tips.

3. **Before you go** online, decide if you are looking for a specialist or a general practitioner.

   _____ online, decide if you are looking for a specialist or a general practitioner.

4. **Before you look**, decide how important the doctor's gender, age, and location are.

   _____ , decide how important the doctor's gender, age, and location are.

5. **While you are searching**, notice the physician's specialty, where he or she attended medical school, and how long he or she has been practicing.

   _____ , notice the physician's specialty, where he or she attended medical school, and how long he or she has been practicing.

6. **While you are studying** the information that you find online, keep in mind that there is a great deal of inaccurate information on the Internet.

   _____ the information that you find online, keep in mind that there is a great deal of inaccurate information on the Internet.

7. **When they are researching** physicians online, many people visit doctor-rating sites.

   _____ physicians online, many people visit doctor-rating sites.

8. **When you are reading** doctor-rating sites, remember that you are reading people's opinions, and not facts.

   _____ doctor-rating sites, remember that you are reading people's opinions, and not facts.

9. **After they do** research online, many people consult social media websites to get further information about the doctor they have chosen.

   _____ research online, many people consult social media websites to get further information about the doctor they have chosen.

10. A study showed that **after they found** a doctor online using social media sites, most people were happy with their choice.

    A study showed that _____ a doctor online using social media sites, most people were happy with their choice.

2 Rewrite the words in bold as reduced adverb clauses.

1. **After she had suffered** for several weeks, the patient finally decided to get help.

   Having suffered for several weeks, the patient finally decided to get help.

2. **After she had had** a bad experience with a doctor in the past, the patient was hesitant to see a physician about her problem.

   _____ a bad experience with a doctor in the past, the patient was hesitant to see a physician about her problem.

3. **After she had consulted** a physician who could not help her, she wasn't sure any doctor could help.

   _____ a physician who could not help her, she wasn't sure any doctor could help.

4. **After she had spoken** with her friends about her condition, she finally decided to see a new doctor.

   _____ with her friends about her condition, she finally decided to see a new doctor.

5. **After she had received** doctor recommendations from several friends, she was ready to choose a new physician.

   _____ doctor recommendations from several friends, she was ready to choose a new physician.

6. **After she had found** a new doctor, she finally made an appointment.

   _____ a new doctor, she finally made an appointment.

3 Write sentences about an experience you had finding a doctor. Use reduced adverb clauses with *when*, *while*, *before*, and *after*.

1. *While searching for a new doctor, I visited several websites that rate doctors.*

2. _____

   _____

3. _____

   _____

4. _____

   _____

Common Vocabulary to Describe Problems and Solutions

1 Complete the sentences about fighting fatigue. Use the words in the box. Sometimes more than one answer is possible, and you will use some words more than once.

by	for	of	to	in

There are several ways _to_ address the problem _____ fatigue. The solution
(1)   (2)

_____ the problem lies _____ the patients themselves. One solution _____
(3)   (4)   (5)

fatigue would be to get more exercise. The problem _____ fatigue can also often be
(6)

solved _____ changes in diet. Medication is another possible solution _____ the
(7)   (8)

problem _____ fatigue.
(9)

considered	necessary

In some cases of extreme fatigue, certain medical conditions must be _____ .
(10)

Medication may be _____ if the patient has a hormonal condition such as a
(11)

malfunctioning thyroid. Major lifestyle changes should be _____ for many patients
(12)

suffering from fatigue. Psychotherapy is _____ in some cases of fatigue.
(13)

secondary	possible	primary

Reduced functioning in a patient's personal life is the _____ issue with fatigue.
(14)

However, a _____ issue is poor work performance. When people experience fatigue,
(15)

they are likely to perform poorly at work. Fatigue may stem from an overtiring job itself.

A _____ solution to this problem is for the patient to reconsider his or her work
(16)

situation. A reduced workload may have very positive effects on a patient's body and mind.

2 Complete the sentences about Internet addiction. Write the correct form of the verbs in parentheses.

1. There _are_ several ways to _address_ the problem of Internet addiction. (address, be)

2. One solution to Internet addiction _____ to _____ the number of hours you _____ online. (be, spend, limit)

3. Another solution _____ to _____ your computer to an uncomfortable location, such as the garage. (move, be)

4. The problem of Internet addiction can often _____ by having a friend or relative _____ your use. (solve, monitor)

5. If the problem of Internet addiction _____ severe, therapy _____ a possible solution. (be, become)

6. An exercise program _____ for many people who _____ from Internet addiction. (consider, suffer)

3 On a separate piece of paper, write three sentences making recommendations of possible solutions. Use the problems in the list and the phrases in the box.

is needed/necessary	should be considered
might/may be considered	must be considered

Problems

cyberchondria   the high cost of medical care

inaccurate information on the Internet   your own ideas

The fact that you may come across inaccurate information should be

considered before taking the advice on websites.

Avoid Common Mistakes

1 Circle the mistakes.

1. Some physicians do not want their patients **to feel** anxious (**so that**) they **give** them a list

   (a)   (b)   (c)

   of medical websites.

2. **The** problem of **the** hypochondria can sometimes **be** solved with medication.

   (a)   (b)   (c)

3. Many physical problems can **be** **caused** by anxiety. **For examples**, headaches
   _(a) _(b) _(c)
   and fatigue.

4. One can **find** reliable **information** on certain sites, **for examples**, sites with URLs
   _(a) _(b) _(c)
   ending in ".gov" or ".edu."

5. Many physicians want **to spend** their consultation time more efficiently **so that** they
   _(a) _(b)
   use e-mail to communicate with patients.
   _(c)

6. **The** problem of **the** cyberchondria is **a result of** patients having too much access
   _(a) _(b) _(c)
   to information.

7. **The** problem of **the** Internet addiction did not **exist** 30 years ago.
   _(a) _(b) _(c)

8. The patient **wasn't able** to reduce his Internet use on his own, **so that** he started
   _(a) _(b)
   therapy **to fight** his addiction.
   _(c)

2 Identify the common mistakes in the sentences. Label each sentence with the type of mistake from the box. If there is no mistake, write *d*. Then correct each sentence.

> a. Remember that *for example* is always singular, even when several examples follow.
> b. Remember that the phrase *The problem of* is not followed by *the*.
> c. Remember not to confuse *so that* (to express purpose) and *so* (to express result).
> d. There is no mistake.

b There are many solutions to the problem of ~~the~~ anxiety. _____ For examples,
₍₁₎ ₍₂₎
removing the causes of stress in one's life and making small lifestyle changes can greatly

help anxiety sufferers. _____ The first step is to try to identify the causes of anxiety so the
₍₃₎
individual can determine whether they can be eliminated. _____ For examples, unpleasant
₍₄₎
working conditions and not having enough money are two common causes of stress. _____
₍₅₎
While individuals may not be able to quit their jobs, counseling may help anxiety sufferers,

giving them strategies so they can cope better with difficult situations. _____ People
₍₆₎
with financial problems can learn money-management techniques so they eliminate

that particular source of stress. _____ The problem of the anxiety can also be solved by
₍₇₎
changing one's lifestyle. _____ For examples, regular exercise and a healthy diet can help
₍₈₎
eliminate stress. _____ Exercise is often relaxing, so that it alleviates stress. _____ Avoiding
₍₉₎ ₍₁₀₎
certain foods and drinks that may lead to anxiety, for examples, caffeinated beverages and

sugary foods, can also help reduce anxiety.

Self-Assessment

Circle the word or phrase that correctly completes each sentence.

1. The students are learning how to evaluate websites _____ they can avoid inaccurate information.

   a. so as to   b. to   c. so

2. Some people look at medical websites _____ to be better informed.

   a. in order   b. so that   c. so

3. _____ use consultation time more efficiently, some doctors have their patients fill out forms online.

   a. So   b. In order to   c. So that

4. The patient didn't want to spend a lot of time at the doctor's office, _____ she made a list of questions before the appointment.

   a. so as to   b. so that   c. so

5. The doctor learned Spanish _____ communicate better with some of her patients.

   a. to   b. so that   c. so

6. _____ that they can understand their patients better, many physicians study "bedside manner."

   a. To   b. So   c. In order to

7. Before _____ online, decide what you are looking for.

   a. going   b. to go   c. you are going

8. While _____ for a new doctor, she consulted many doctor-rating websites.

   a. to look   b. look   c. looking

9. Having _____ many people, she finally found a new physician.

   a. seen   b. seeing   c. see

10. Having _____ the symptoms online, she began to worry.

    a. find   b. found   c. finding

11. One solution _____ the problem of obesity is to increase the number of physical education classes in the schools.

    a. by   b. to   c. of

12. The high cost of medical care must _____ .

    a. be needed   b. be considered   c. consider

13. If a cold or the flu lasts for several days, _____ to see a doctor.

    a. necessary   b. it is needed   c. it may be necessary

14. There are many solutions to _____ cyberchondria.

    a. the problem of   b. the problem   c. the problem of the

15. There are many signs of cyberchondria. _____ , a patient may be anxious or argumentative.

    a. An example   b. For example   c. For examples

Problem–Solution 4

Leading a Healthy Life

It Constructions

1 Unscramble the sentences about diet and exercise from a health class.

1. to / it / extend / by choosing healthier foods / your life / possible / may be

   It may be possible to extend your life by choosing healthier foods.

2. it / to / might be / your diet / difficult / change

   _____

3. might not work / is / that / possible / a diet / it

   _____

4. too much / be / exercise / may not / helpful / it / to do

   _____

5. are / it / that / seems / the first weeks of a diet / very difficult

   _____

6. be / some foods / it / our memories / might / true / that / strengthen

   _____

7. that / enough nutrients / it / is / do not provide / true / some vegetables

   _____

8. appears / energy levels / healthy eating / that / it / improves

   _____

9. that people should eat / five servings of fruit and vegetables a day / it seems

   _____

2 Complete the sentences about herbal remedies. Use *that*, *to*, or *for*.

1. It is possible _to_ treat some illnesses with herbs.

2. It is sometimes difficult _____ people to find natural herbs in stores.

3. It is likely _____ some herbal remedies are from ancient times.

4. It is easy _____ forget that some herbs are poisonous.

5. It is true _____ some doctors don't approve of herbal remedies.

6. It seems _____ some people trust herbal remedies more than antibiotics.

7. It is hard _____ some people to accept herbal remedies as legitimate medicine.

8. It is difficult _____ prepare some herbal medicines at home.

9. It is essential _____ research herbal medicines before taking them.

10. It is important _____ follow the directions on the packaging.

11. It is unlikely _____ herbal medicine will replace conventional medicine.

12. It is evident _____ some herbs are effective in treating certain ailments.

3 Complete the sentences about the benefits of vitamins using *it* constructions. Use an infinitive or *that* clause and the word in parentheses.

1. _It is important to_ boost your immune system with Vitamin C. (important)

2. _____ Vitamin A prevents or decreases flu symptoms. (appear)

3. _____ absorb Vitamin D in the winter. (difficult)

4. _____ people will get the flu in the summer months. (unlikely)

5. _____ Vitamin B6 helps the nervous system. (seem)

6. _____ people seek advice from their doctor before taking new vitamins. (best)

7. _____ prevent anemia by taking iron. (possible)

8. _____ Vitamin K interacts badly with some medicines. (appear)

9. _____ some vitamins taken in the correct dosage are beneficial. (certain)

10. _____ boost your immune system by eating properly and getting lots of sleep. (easy)

11. _____ regular exercise makes people feel healthier and happier. (true)

12. _____ people should limit the amount of junk food they consume. (obvious)

4 Rewrite the sentences. Use a passive voice *it* construction for the words in bold.

1. **Researchers have found** that vegetarians often lack sufficient iron in their diets.

   It has been found that vegetarians often lack sufficient iron in their diets.

2. **Doctors suggest** that people with allergies to dairy products drink soy milk.

   _____ that people with allergies to dairy products drink soy milk.

3. **People believe** that diets high in sugar and fat are very unhealthy.

   _____ that diets high in sugar and fat are very unhealthy.

4. **Doctors have proven** that diets high in fiber are good for the digestive system.

   _____ that diets high in fiber are good for the digestive system.

5. **Researchers can show** that artificial sweeteners have negative effects on animals.

   _____ that artificial sweeteners have negative effects on animals.

6. **Doctors have found** that patients who followed vegan diets had healthy hearts.

   _____ that patients who followed vegan diets had healthy hearts.

7. **People think** that gluten-free diets are difficult to follow.

   _____ that gluten-free diets are difficult to follow.

8. **People accept** that some people follow strictly vegetarian diets.

   _____ that some people follow strictly vegetarian diets.

9. **Scientists have found** that certain vegetables and fruits have anticancer properties.

   _____ that certain vegetables and fruits have anticancer properties.

5 Complete the sentences. Write about healthy eating habits. Use your own ideas.

1. It may be true that *vitamins are good for you, but I think they should be*
   taken in moderation .

2. It could be argued that _____ .

3. It might seem that _____ .

4. It's important to _____ .

5. It's essential to _____ .

Common Transition Words to Indicate Steps of a Solution

1 Read the web article about the treatment of dehydration in the body. Then label the purpose of each word or phrase in bold.

A = to introduce the first step	C = to indicate steps happening at the same time
B = to introduce additional steps	D = to conclude the process

Living Without **Water**

Dehydration is a very serious issue around the world for children, athletes, and others who may be susceptible to it. _A_ **First**, there has to be a reason for the process to begin,
(1)
whether it is an illness causing loss of fluids, or extreme physical activity in hot weather.

_____ **At the same time**, the lost fluid is not being replaced at all, or is not being replaced
(2)
quickly enough. Dehydration _____ **then** continues, and physical signs become obvious.
(3)
What physical signs are evident during the process of dehydration? _____ **To begin**,
(4)
the person may get a headache, or the face may turn red. _____ **After that**, the symptoms
(5)
may become more unusual, for example an inability to drink, or crying with no tears.

_____ **Following that**, the symptoms become more severe, including fainting, extreme
(6)
muscle cramping, or rapid heart rate. _____ **Last**, the person may go into shock, which is a
(7)
serious medical condition. The person could die from shock.

As soon as these more severe symptoms appear, it is extremely important to seek urgent medical care and monitor the person as he or she receive fluids.

2 Read the informational flier about the process of finding a personal trainer. Complete the sentences with a word or phrase from the box. Capitalize the first word of the sentence when necessary.

after that	second	third	Ø
last	then	~~to begin~~	

In their efforts to get fit, many people seek help from a personal trainer, but finding a personal trainer can be difficult. In order to find a good trainer, consider using a systematic approach. _To begin_ , ask family and friends for recommendations. If this
(1)
fails, ask for a recommendation at a local gym. _____ , schedule an appointment
(2)
just to meet the trainer, not to begin training. _____ , interview the trainer about
(3)
the training programs he or she uses, including types of exercises, diets, and any other parts of the training program. If the trainer seems like a good match, you should _____ ask about his or her education and certification. _____ It is very
(4)   (5)
important that you choose someone who has been educated and licensed to train you. _____ , you will want to discuss specific details of your program, including
(6)
rates, and develop a detailed program, together with your trainer, that you can follow. _____ , begin your program and find a healthier you!
(7)

3 Read the sentences about choosing a doctor. Write a paragraph on the next page using the sentences with transition words to indicate the process.

1. Decide whether you prefer a male or a female doctor.

2. Ask friends and family for recommendations.

3. Contact the doctors' offices to find out about their hours, rates, and the insurance plans they accept.

4. Make a list of questions to ask the doctors.

5. Make an appointment to interview the doctors and then ask your questions.

6. Choose a doctor based on the interviews.

7. If you already have a doctor, notify him or her that you would like to have your records forwarded to the new doctor.

_____
_____
_____
_____
_____
_____
_____
_____
_____
_____
_____

Avoid Common Mistakes

1 Circle the mistakes.

1. **It is important to** monitor calorie intake. First list the foods you eat. **Than** estimate
   (a)   (b)   (c)
   how much you eat.

2. **It is impossible Ø** underestimate the effects of first overeating and **then** failing
   (a)   (b)   (c)
   to exercise.

3. **It is importand to** first talk to your doctor. **Then** you can start a diet you agree on.
   (a)   (b)   (c)

4. **It is often impossible convince** some people that **it is important to** exercise.
   (a)   (b)   (c)

5. **It is important to** see a doctor once a year, and **it is also import** to go to the dentist.
   (a)   (b)   (c)

6. As we age, our hearing may deteriorate first and **then** our eyesight, but **it's impossible**
   (a)   (b)

   Ø us to predict how severe the loss will be.
   (c)

7. **It is important to** see a doctor, but it may be impossible **Ø** convince sick people to
   (a)   (b)   (c)
   do so.

8. **It is important to** schedule your day well and **than** get enough sleep at night.
   (a)   (b)   (c)

2 Identify the common mistakes in the sentences. Label each sentence with the type of mistake from the box. If there is no mistake, write *d*. Then correct each sentence.

a. Remember to use *It is important to* and not *It is import to* or *It is importand to*.	c. Remember to use *then*, and not *than*, when introducing next steps.
b. Remember to use *to* or *for* after *impossible*.	d. There is no mistake.

important

_*a*_ According to a research study at a major American university, it is very ~~import~~
(1)

to have a good attitude in order to stay healthy. _____ For many people, it is impossible
(2)

believe that our attitudes can affect our health, but this seems to be true. _____ Most
(3)

people understand that it is importand to be positive in order to be happy. _____
(4)

According to researchers, a positive attitude first lowers blood pressure and than other

positive effects follow, such as healthier blood flow and heart rate. _____ These findings are
(5)

noteworthy because it is important to remember that heart health has a strong influence

on overall health. _____ Although it is impossible researchers to measure exactly how
(6)

much a positive attitude can benefit the heart, it is definitely significant. _____ So, the next
(7)

time you are feeling upset, remind yourself of the results of this study, than take a deep

breath and try to relax.

Self-Assessment

Circle the word or phrase that correctly completes each sentence.

1. It is difficult _____ some people to discuss their health problems with others.

   a. to   b. for   c. that

2. It _____ that the portion sizes in American restaurants are too large.

   a. suggest   b. suggested   c. has been suggested

3. _____ , the nurse will take your temperature. Then he will check your blood pressure.

   a. To begin   b. Last   c. Third

4. It is impossible _____ know how long someone will live.

   a. to   b. for   c. that

5. It is not recommended _____ chicken at a dinner that vegetarians will attend.

   a. serving   b. to serve   c. serve

6. If you are in an accident, first make sure you are all right. You can _____ get out of the car if it is safe to do so.

   a. after that   b. last   c. then

7. When dieting, it is helpful to write what you ate as soon as you are finished eating. _____ , make a note of any items that you can eliminate next time to cut calories.

   a. At the same time   b. As soon as   c. First

8. It is advisable _____ you go to the hospital if you get a serious burn.

   a. to   b. for   c. that

9. When storing fresh food, first choose a container, then put the food in and close it immediately. _____ , store the container in the refrigerator.

   a. Than   b. To begin   c. Finally

10. It _____ that women who felt comfortable with their doctors had fewer health problems.

    a. were found   b. was found   c. found

11. It is useful _____ the phone numbers of your dentist and doctor in your phone's contact list.

    a. to keep   b. keeping   c. kept

12. During an emergency, _____ call for an ambulance. Then attend to any people who are hurt.

    a. following that   b. first   c. last

13. It may be possible _____ a long time even with very advanced cancer.

    a. to live   b. that lived   c. have lived

14. It is often difficult _____ poor people to afford fresh fruits and vegetables.

    a. to   b. for   c. that

15. To lose weight, first talk to your doctor. _____ , you should follow the doctor's instructions.

    a. In the end   b. After that   c. Third

Summary–Response
Privacy in the Digital Age

Past Unreal Conditionals

1 Complete the sentences about using computers at work. Write the correct form of the verbs in parentheses. Use past unreal conditionals.

1. If _you hadn't used_ (not / use) the computer to play games, your manager _wouldn't_

   have been (not / be) upset.

2. Your computer _____ (be) safe from attack if you _____ (sign) out.

3. If you _____ (not / open) that file, a virus _____ (not / infect)

   the network.

4. The network security team _____ (not / contact) you if you

   _____ (not / report) that virus.

5. If you _____ (not / spend) so much time reading blogs, you

   _____ (finish) your report.

6. If you _____ (close) your personal e-mail, your manager

   _____ (not / see) it.

2 Circle the sentence that expresses true information about the past unreal conditional statement.

1. If she had used a surge protector, she wouldn't have damaged her computer.

   a. Her computer is fine.

   b. Her computer is damaged.

   c. She used a surge protector.

2. Blanca wouldn't have been a victim of identity theft if she had not entered her credit card information on a strange website.

   a. Blanca was a victim of identity theft.

   b. Blanca didn't enter information on a strange website.

   c. Blanca was not a victim of identity theft.

3. His laptop wouldn't have broken if it had been in a case.

   a. His laptop was in a case.

   b. His laptop fell out of a case.

   c. His laptop broke.

4. If Joe had used only one credit card online, thieves wouldn't have gotten the numbers of all three of his credit cards.

   a. Joe only had one credit card.

   b. Joe only used one credit card online.

   c. Joe used more than one credit card online.

5. If Mary had used a stronger password, hackers might not have been able to figure it out.

   a. Hackers weren't able to figure out Mary's password.

   b. Mary didn't use a strong password.

   c. Mary told hackers her password.

6. If Tina had logged out of her account, other people wouldn't have been able to use it.

   a. Tina didn't log out of her account.

   b. Others weren't able to use Tina's account.

   c. Tina logged out of her account.

7. If Luis had charged his laptop, it wouldn't have shut down while he was making a purchase.

   a. The computer didn't shut down.

   b. The computer was charged.

   c. The computer wasn't charged.

8. If Akiko had had a Wi-Fi connection, she could have been able to send the report.

   a. Akiko didn't have a Wi-Fi connection.

   b. Akiko sent the report.

   c. Akiko had a Wi-Fi connection.

9. If Pietro hadn't forgotten his username, he could have bought the tickets he wants online.

   a. Pietro didn't forget his username.

   b. Pietro bought the tickets online.

   c. Pietro forgot his username.

10. If I had bought a smartphone, I wouldn't have needed to take a laptop on my trip.

   a. I bought a smartphone.

   b. I didn't buy a smartphone.

   c. I didn't bring a laptop.

3 Unscramble the sentences about privacy and technology. Add commas when necessary.

1. If / we would have responded / they had texted us

   If they had texted us, we would have responded.

2. If / your number / I had recognized / the phone / I would have answered

   _____

3. you wouldn't have gotten / you had visited / only trusted websites / the computer virus / If

   _____

4. Murat hadn't given his number to strangers / he wouldn't have received / If / prank phone calls

   _____

5. on strange links / If / you wouldn't have had problems / you hadn't clicked

   _____

6. I would have received / your e-mail / If / I had logged on

   _____

7. if / You couldn't have / protected your password very well / your e-mail was hacked

   _____

8. online / the money / used your credit card / if you hadn't / you wouldn't have lost

   _____

9. had been more patient / If / your laptop / wouldn't have crashed / you

_____

10. the news report online / we wouldn't have known / If / about the scam / we hadn't seen

_____

4 Complete the sentences about technology. Write sentences that are true for you. Use past unreal conditionals.

1. If the Internet had never been invented, _I would have spent more money on_

   stamps last year.

2. If cell phones had never been developed, _____

   _____ .

3. If I hadn't learned how to use a computer, _____

   _____ .

4. If social media hadn't been created, _____

   _____ .

5. If e-mail hadn't existed, _____

   _____ .

Common Phrases Used in Summary–Response Writing

1 Read Ingrid's summary–response paper about an article on safely using a public Wi-Fi network. Underline the phrases of summary–response writing. Then label each phrase.

> A = introduces and identifies the ideas of the original text
> B = indicates what the author omitted or did not consider
> C = concludes the summary

_A_ (1) The article "Protecting Yourself in Public" provides valuable information on how to protect important personal information when using public Wi-Fi networks.

_A_ (2) According to the author, Wi-Fi networks in libraries, coffee shops, and airports are convenient, but can be dangerous because others may have an easier time accessing sensitive information. _A_ (3) The author further explains that it is often the actions of the victim that lead the individual to become a victim. _A_ (4) The author goes on to show how people don't realize that when checking their e-mail, their password may be observed, making it possible for others to access the account. _C_ (5) The author concludes that using only secure computers for things such as online shopping and banking is the only way to protect oneself.

_B_ (6) The author fails to address the fact that, for economic reasons, many people do not have access to a secure computer. _B_ (7) The author does not mention that, for some individuals, their work schedules are such that they have to do business in an airport. _C_ (8) Furthermore, the author fails to provide useful advice for those who are most likely to be harmed by such actions.

2 Read the beginning of Daniel's summary–response paper on an article about identifying fraudulent e-mails. Write the word or phrase from the box that best completes each sentence. Sometimes more than one answer may be possible.

~~addresses~~	starts	concludes	goes on to give
also says	states	fails to address	summing up

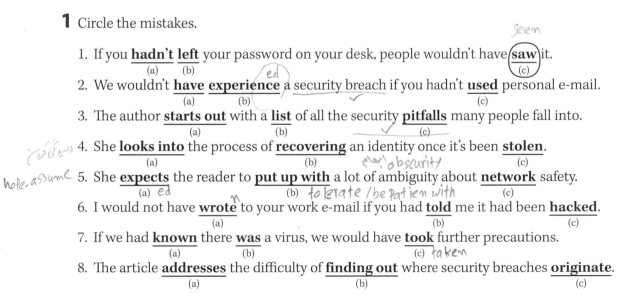

Emily Black, the director of the Online Consumer Protection Foundation, _addresses_ the issue of fraudulent e-mails and how to identify them in an article
(1)
entitled "More Than a Simple Request" (2011). She ___starts___ her article
(2)
by explaining that thousands of people fall victim to online scams involving e-mail.

She _also says_ that there are ways that consumers can recognize fraudulent
(3)
e-mails and protect themselves from them. She _goes on to give_ several examples
(4)
of ways to recognize these e-mails, including looking for spelling errors and odd
return e-mail addresses. The article ___states___ when people should inform law
(5)
enforcement about fraudulent e-mails. Black _concludes_ the article with a list
(6)
of agencies that counsel consumers who have been harmed by fraudulent e-mails.

Summing up, this article is helpful, but it did not go far enough. For example, the
(7)
author _fails to address_ some of the most common tricks that criminals use to gain
(8)
access to passwords, such as launching spyware through seemingly innocent links.

3 Read an article or text of your choice. On a separate piece of paper, summarize it using the summary–response phrases from Ingrid and Daniel's essays. Then respond using appropriate phrases to express agreement or disagreement.

Avoid Common Mistakes

1 Circle the mistakes.

1. If you **hadn't** **left** your password on your desk, people wouldn't have **saw** it.
   (a)   (b)   (c)
2. We wouldn't **have** **experience** a security breach if you hadn't **used** personal e-mail.
   (a)   (b)   (c)
3. The author **starts out** with a **list** of all the security **pitfalls** many people fall into.
   (a)   (b)   (c)
4. She **looks into** the process of **recovering** an identity once it's been **stolen**.
   (a)   (b)   (c)
5. She **expects** the reader to **put up with** a lot of ambiguity about **network** safety.
   (a)   (b)   (c)
6. I would not have **wrote** to your work e-mail if you had **told** me it had been **hacked**.
   (a)   (b)   (c)
7. If we had **known** there **was** a virus, we would have **took** further precautions.
   (a)   (b)   (c)
8. The article **addresses** the difficulty of **finding out** where security breaches **originate**.
   (a)   (b)   (c)

2 Identify the common mistakes in the sentences. Label each sentence with the type of mistake from the box. If there is no mistake, write *c*. Then correct each sentence.

> a. Remember to use the past participle form of the verb after the modal in past unreal conditional sentences.
>
> b. Remember to use academic, precise words rather than multi-word verbs or idioms.
>
> c. There is no mistake.

_b_ In her article on how companies use social media in the hiring process, Sarah
(1)
                    investigates
Valero-Preston ~~looks into~~ the ethical issues as well as the practical ones of such

investigations. _b_ Valero-Preston starts out with a description of the things that
(2)

companies are concerned about. _c_ She then explains how companies use
(3)

investigators to search for relevant information about the job applicants. _c_ If many
(4)

job seekers had understood how their personal comments on blogs could hurt them,

they probably would have took more time in choosing their words. _c_ According to
(5)

the author, the job seekers must consent to the process before anyone can look into

their social media history. _c_ Of course, the investigators start out with the popular
(6)

social media sites, but they also search even deeper for comments on these sites

and less well-known ones. _b_ If some applicants had known about such extensive
(7)

searches, Valero-Preston wonders if they would have consented. _c_ The author
(8)

wraps up by reminding us that the Internet is a public space, and anyone can search

your name.

Self-Assessment

Circle the word or phrase that correctly completes each sentence.

1. If you hadn't made those comments on social media sites, the company would have _____ you.

   a. hire   (b.) hired   c. hiring

2. I'm not certain, but you _____ have been able to stop the investigation if you had confessed.

   a. might   (b.) would   c. couldn't

3. The authors _____ the article by making recommendations for further research in the field.

    a. wrap up   b. conclude   c. further state

4. The author has failed to _____ the realities of using social media at work.

    a. address   b. not mention   c. start

5. If we _____ the document, we would not have lost so much data.

    a. save   b. saved   c. had saved

6. The investigators would not have _____ your comments if you had used a different username.

    a. find   b. found   c. founded

7. _____ the author, social media sites are not always as private as we think.

    a. Summing up   b. Discussing   c. According to

8. Many people would not _____ having their Internet history searched in order to secure a job.

    a. put up with   b. tolerate   c. stand for

9. The company would not _____ any evidence to fire you if you hadn't used your work e-mail.

    a. have had   b. had had   c. have been having

10. _____ , the author didn't prove that networks are more secure today than they were last year.

    a. According to   b. In conclusion   c. Wrapping up

11. If we _____ our password, hackers would have continued using our account.

    a. hadn't changed   b. had changed   c. changed

12. The author _____ that online banking is very safe. He then discusses the merits of it.

    a. sums up   b. quotes   c. further states

13. If you hadn't explained the security process to me, I wouldn't have _____ .

    a. understand   b. understood   c. understanding

14. The author _____ the subject in depth.

    a. notes that   b. goes on to explain   c. concludes that

15. If I _____ my phone, I would have texted you sooner.

    a. hadn't lost   b. was lost   c. didn't lose

Persuasion 1

Violence in the Media

Nonidentifying Relative Clauses in Persuasive Writing

1 Underline the relative clauses in the sentences about violence in the media. Then label each sentence. Add commas when necessary.

> NI = nonidentifying   I = identifying
>
> *[handwritten: non Sr   Sen]*

1. _NI_ Our sociology professor, <u>who is also the father of three</u>, believes that violence in movies has created a less sensitive population.

2. _NI_ According to our professor, violent movies, <u>which are quite popular today,</u> have not had positive effects on many children.

3. _NI_ Our class spoke to Dr. Samantha Smith, <u>who is a psychology professor,</u> about the effects of movie violence on teenagers.

4. _NI_ Dr. Smith says that violence, which is portrayed as funny, is particularly offensive to parents.

5. _NI_ She reports that many children, who are younger than 17, regularly see violent movies with older siblings or friends.

6. _NI_ Dr. Smith's children, who are both between the ages of 6 and 10, are not permitted to watch violent movies.

7. _NI_ Dr. Henry Brown, whose mother is also a researcher, is known for conducting studies about the effect of violence on children.

8. _NI_ Dr. Brown has found that movies, which show women and children in frightening situations, are extremely disturbing to many people.

2 Complete the sentences about Olga's brothers. Use *whose, who, which,* or Ø. Then label each clause *NI* (for nonidentifying adjective clause) or *A* (for appositive).

1. _NI_ My parents have activated the parental controls on our only television, _which_ is located in the living room.

2. _NI_ *[APP]* My aunt, _who is_ Ø a parent of three boys, feels strongly about preventing her children from watching violent television shows.

3. N\ My aunt's best friend, _whose_ child is permitted to watch anything, is not nearly so strict about violent television shows.

4. N\ My brothers, _who_ are always trying to turn off the parental controls, often argue with my parents about television shows.

5. N\ Their favorite shows, _whose_ names I can't recall, are sometimes violent.

App 6. N\ Sometimes my brothers visit Kevin, _∅_ the son of my aunt's friend, when they want to watch TV.

7. N\ My parents' opinions, _which_ do not seem to matter to my brothers, aren't enough to change their behavior.

8. N\ My opinion, _which_ is the same as my aunt's, is that my parents should not permit my brothers to go to Kevin's house.

3 Complete the blog post about Bryant's child psychology professors. Use the appropriate clause from the box.

a child advocacy organization	a very popular children's television show
all psychology majors	located in the center of campus
an expert on child psychology	work appears in many respected journals
difficult to write	writes extensively on child psychology

Semester Update 1

I am enjoying my semester so far. Alex Mason is my professor. Professor Mason, who

is _an expert on child psychology_ , has written two books on the effects of television
          (1)

on children. You can get a copy of her book at the university's psychology research

center, which is _located_ . Dr. Victoria Holcomb,
                    (2)

who _writes extensively on child_ , is also a professor at this university.
        (3)

Professor Holcomb, whose _work_ , often conducts
                           (4)

joint research with Professor Mason. The Foundation for Child Safety, which is

difficult to write , has funded much of their research on the
        (5)

effects of violence on children. Last semester, Professors Mason and Holcomb conducted

research on _Action Heroes and Villains_, which is _a very_ .
                                            (6)

My classmates and I, who are _all_ , helped them write
                             (7)

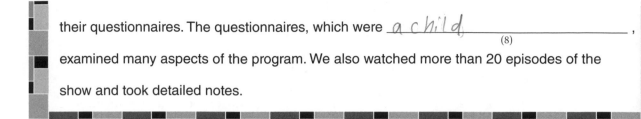

their questionnaires. The questionnaires, which were _a child,_ _____ ,
(8)

examined many aspects of the program. We also watched more than 20 episodes of the

show and took detailed notes.

4 Read the press release. Then write new sentences by adding the additional information, using nonidentifying relative clauses.

1. Families United Against Violence has organized a conference for youth.
   Additional information: Families United Against Violence is a local nonprofit group.

   Families United Against Violence, which is a local nonprofit group, has

   organized a conference for youth.

2. Dr. Susan Smith will be giving a lecture on media violence at this conference.
   Additional information: Dr. Susan Smith's research is groundbreaking.

   _____

3. *Captain Hero* is going to stop creating violent story lines.
   Additional information: Captain Hero is a popular children's show.

   _____

4. Nick Robinson is presenting a series of interviews from the conference.
   Additional information: Nick Robinson is a nationally recognized reporter.

   _____

5. Theresa Filmore will be speaking at the conference.
   Additional information: Theresa Filmore is an award-winning journalist.

   _____

6. *Time* will probably cover the conference.
   Additional information: Time is an American news magazine.

   _____

7. Americans Against Violence organized a similar conference last year.
   Additional information: Americans Against Violence is a grassroots community group.

   _____

8. Josh Willow has become president of this organization.
   Additional information: Josh Willow is a star high school athlete and scholar.

   _____

Phrases That Limit Overgeneralization

1 Unscramble the sentences about violence in movies. Add punctuation when necessary.

1. young people / most violence in movies / to involve / tends

   Most violence in movies tends to involve young people.

2. are / watch / likely to / older people / dramatic or comedic movies

   _____

3. action movies / seems that / it / popular / are / with young people

   _____

4. the villain in a horror movie / people / to hate / tend

   _____

5. comedic movies / than violent movies / tend / more appealing / to be

   _____

6. appears that / is / it / the action movie / the best one in theaters now

   _____

7. seem / horror movies / weak plots and character development / to have

   _____

8. in most cases / roles in violent movies / avoid / my favorite actors

   _____

9. their fear of frightening movies / hide / typically / young teens

   _____

10. many reviewers / more critical of the acting in violent movies / tend / to be

    _____

11. appear / violent movies / shorter than nonviolent ones / to be

    _____

12. one news source / very worried / violence in popular movies / according to / about / parents are

    _____

2 Rewrite the sentences from a newspaper editorial. Use the expressions in parentheses to make them less generalized.

Have your say . . .

1. Teens who listen to heavy metal **are** more disrespectful to their parents and authority figures. (be likely to)

   Teens who listen to heavy metal _are likely to be_ more disrespectful to their parents and authority figures.

2. Heavy metal bands **attract** teens that have trouble with their parents. (tend to)

   Heavy metal bands _____ teens that have trouble with their parents.

3. Teens who play music **cope** well with stress in their lives. (typically)

   Teens who play music _____ well with stress in their lives.

4. Violent lyrics in songs **have** a negative impact on teens. (mainly)

   Violent lyrics in songs _____ a negative impact on teens.

5. Parents who have positive relationships with their families **do not allow** their children to listen to music with violent lyrics. (appear not to)

   Parents who have positive relationships with their families _____ their children to listen to music with violent lyrics.

6. Violent music **is** louder and faster than nonviolent music. (be likely)

   Violent music _____ louder and faster than nonviolent music.

7. Students who listen to violent music **are** less likely to have stable social lives. (seem to)

   Students who listen to violent music _____ less likely to have stable social lives.

8. Uplifting music **is** more popular with well-adjusted people. (appear to)

   Uplifting music _____ more popular with well-adjusted people.

9. Young people who listen to folk music or country music **do** well in school. (tend to)

   Young people who listen to folk music or country music _____ well in school.

Avoid Common Mistakes

1 Circle the mistakes.

1. It **seem** that afternoon cartoons, **which** strongly influence children, are in need of
   (a)   (b)
   regulation. However, advertisers **that** sponsor kids' TV shows do not always agree.
                                     (c)

2. Although a particular TV show may **seem** innocent, **it** may be a good idea for parents
                                      (a)   (b)
   to watch it. They need to understand its influence, **that** may not be obvious, on
                                                        (c)
   their children.

3. The articles from the *Herald-Sun*, **Ø** is the local newspaper, **seem** to be written by
                                        (a)   (b)
   people with credentials **that** are very impressive.
                           (c)

4. Late-night television shows, **that** are intended for mature audiences, are the ones **that**
                                 (a)   (b)
   usually scare me so much **that** I can't sleep.
                            (c)

5. My psychology professors **seem** to respect the research **that** was funded by the
                            (a)   (b)
   National Education Foundation, **Ø** is headquartered here.
                                  (c)

6. It **seem** that the Society of Motion Picture Directors, **which** most movie directors
      (a)   (b)
   belong to, believes that the degrees of violence in movies **seem** to be difficult to
                                                              (c)
   define consistently.

7. The family-viewing hour, **Ø** is an hour of nonviolent television, **seems** to be unpopular
                            (a)   (b)
   with some people **who** are younger.
                    (c)

8. Advocates for a Violence-Free Society, **Ø** is a nonprofit organization, **seem** to be
                                          (a)   (b)
   starting a campaign **that** asks senators to pass laws against media violence.
                       (c)

2 Identify the common mistakes in the sentences. Label each sentence with the type of mistake from the box. If there is no mistake, write *d*. Then correct each sentence.

a. Remember to include the relative pronoun in nonidentifying relative clauses.	c. Remember to use the singular form of the verb *seem* with *it*.
b. Remember not to use *that* as a relative pronoun in nonidentifying relative clauses.	d. There is no mistake.

seems
These days _c_ it ~~seem~~ that many parents are concerned about their children's favorite
      (1)

TV shows _____ . Some of these shows include violent images or events, can have a huge
          (2)

impression on young minds. _____ As a result, parents who are upset with the available
                          (3)

shows are taking matters into their own hands. _____ These parents use money, that can
                                               (4)

be a big motivator, to influence advertisers. _____ The angry parents do not simply write
                                              (5)

e-mails and letters, can easily be ignored or lost, but they stop buying those advertisers'

products. _____ They also use social media to coordinate their campaigns, which makes
          (6)

their efforts even more effective. _____ These parents have opponents, but it seem that
                                   (7)

momentum is on the side of the families.

Self-Assessment

Circle the word, phrase, or item that correctly completes each sentence.

1. The professor's interests, _____ are very complicated, are clearly outlined in this article.

   a. Ø   b. that   c. which

2. Violent movies _____ be released more frequently in the summer than in the winter.

   a. seems to   b. seem to   c. seems

3. Kevin Nelson, _____ an award-winning reporter, has recently written an article on violence in our community.

   a. which   b. Ø   c. who

4. Children who watch movies with a positive message _____ be more compassionate.

   a. tend to   b. tend   c. tends to

5. The senator, _____ voted for this bill just last month, is now completely opposed to it.

   a. which   b. who   c. that

6. Violent films, _____ content may affect kids, should be regulated.

   a. which   b. that   c. whose

7. My professor, _____ believes that violent films harm society, says they should be banned.

   a. who   b. whose   c. what

8. My brothers and I _____ to watch violent movies with large groups of friends.

   a. am likely   b. is likely   c. are likely

9. Parents for Safer Kids, _____ nonprofit organization, has begun a letter-writing campaign.

   a. a   b. Ø   c. which

10. It _____ unlikely that anyone can entirely avoid seeing violent television shows.

    a. seem   b. seems   c. Ø

11. _____ that violent movies really do have an influence on behavior.

    a. It seems   b. It's appears   c. It is

12. Stronger laws, _____ are worth discussing, might reduce violence in society.

    a. who   b. that   c. which

13. Tina James, _____ movie director, has made some of the most violent movies I've ever seen.

    a. a   b. which   c. Ø

14. The Concerned Parents Group, _____ encourages stricter media control, will protest today.

    a. Ø   b. which   c. that

15. A person's age and gender _____ have little influence on their preference for movie genres.

    a. appears to   b. appears   c. appear to

Persuasion 2

Living in an Age of Information Overload

Noun Clauses with *Wh-* Words and *If / Whether*

1 Complete the sentences about technology in the workplace. Circle the phrase that correctly completes each sentence.

1. Many employers, and many employees, are interested in _____ their workplaces more flexible.

   a. can modern technology make

   b. how can modern technology make

   ⓒ how modern technology can make

2. Some employers are familiar with the old idea of teleworking, or working from home, but are unsure _____ .

   a. what should today's effective virtual workplace look like

   b. what today's effective virtual workplace should look like

   c. should today's effective virtual workplace look like

3. Forward-thinking companies are trying to decide _____ .

   a. how the wide range of new mobile technologies could benefit their employees

   b. how could the wide range of new mobile technologies benefit their employees

   c. the wide range of new mobile technologies could benefit their employees

4. Employers may not be sure _____ to keep their employees connected.

   a. which devices and equipment they need

   b. which devices and equipment do they need

   c. devices and equipment that they need

5. Employers also need to reflect on _____ , and then make sure their technology facilitates it.

   a. they want their employees to collaborate

   b. how do they want their employees to collaborate

   c. how they want their employees to collaborate

6. Experts will continue to debate _____ .

    a. type of workplace best for business

    b. which type of workplace is best for business

    c. type of workplace which is best for business

7. There is no general agreement on _____ .

    a. should communication technology be used in the workplace

    b. how should communication technology be used in the workplace

    c. how communication technology should be used in the workplace

8. However, because of the flexibility technology allows, employers should consider _____ .

    a. what they can do to take advantage of these exciting new tools

    b. what can they do to take advantage of these exciting new tools

    c. can they do to take advantage of these exciting new tools

2 Rewrite the questions about online courses. Use a noun clause with a *wh-* word to make statements.

1. How do online courses compare to traditional courses?

    Students today often wonder *how online courses compare to traditional courses* .

2. What types of learners are most likely to succeed in an online course?

    Students should look into _____ .

3. How successful are they at working independently?

    Students who are considering an online class should reflect on

    _____ .

4. What types of interactions with classmates do online students have?

    It is often not clear to potential online students _____ .

5. How much teacher time and attention do students receive?

    Before taking an online class, students should consider _____ .

6. How many courses are available online?

    It is not known _____ .

7. Which institutions consider online courses the equivalent of traditional courses?

    It is not always clear _____ .

8. When might taking an online course lead to information overload?

   Students should also consider _____ .

9. How do successful online learners manage electronic distractions while they are trying to study?

   Researchers are interested in _____ .

3 Complete the sentences about how Andrew spends his time online. Match the phrases to correctly complete each sentence.

1. Andrew has been wondering whether _d_ .

2. He often feels stressed, and he isn't sure _____ .

3. He's wondering if _____ .

4. He's asked himself _____ , he should just turn the computer off for the evening.

5. He is starting to focus on _____ he spent less time online.

6. Andrew's wife is not sure if _____ .

7. She is wondering if Andrew _____ .

8. According to her, Andrew needs to start focusing _____ .

a. he would be happier if he limited his time online to a few hours a day

b. Andrew will really be able to make such a big change

c. whether his life would be more rewarding if

d̸. he is suffering from information overload.

e. on whether he is spending enough time with family and friends

f. whether every day at 7 p.m.

g. whether that stress is caused by the amount of time he spends online

h. might shut down the computer and then switch to checking social media sites on his phone

4 Complete the sentences about shopping for technology products. Write sentences that are true for you.

1. Before I buy any new technology, I think about _how useful it is going to be_ .

2. Advertisements can be very persuasive, but I consider whether

   _____ .

3. Before people buy a new device, they should find out _____

   _____ and _____ .

4. To decide whether I can trust an online information source, I always look at

   _____ .

5. Although I love gadgets, I always consider whether _____

   _____ .

Phrases for Argumentation

1 Read the student essays. Label each sentence with the type of statement from the box.

OV = opposing view	R = refutation	TS = thesis statement
AO = acknowledge an opposing argument	SI = supporting information	

Student A

TS E-books should be used in elementary schools. _____ It has been argued that
(1)   (2)
traditional books are more connected to the "reading experience" for young children.

_____ Obviously, traditional books are more economical for large school systems. _____
(3)   (4)
However, it is important for young students to be familiar with and able to use up-to-

date technologies. _____ Children who learn to use advanced technologies when they
(5)
are young will have a big advantage when they are older.

Student B

_____ The most important thing teachers can do in the elementary classroom is
(6)
to spend time interacting with their students. _____ It could be claimed that young
(7)
children should be introduced to the latest technology at school. _____ Clearly, children
(8)
can benefit from early exposure to technology. _____ However, it is simply not true that
(9)
the latest gadgets should be introduced in elementary schools. _____ It is best to let
(10)
children be children, and to introduce the world of technology when they are older.

2 Complete the sentences about distracted driving. Circle the words that correctly complete each sentence.

1. Distracted driving is a type of information overload. _____ , trying to do two things at once overloads the brain.

   a. However   ⓑ Clearly   c. It is not true that

2. _____ most drivers can safely talk on the phone or use a GPS while driving.

   a. It could be argued that   b. That may be so,   c. While it is true that

3. _____ that hands-free use of a cell phone is safer than hand-held use.

   a. Obviously,   b. However   c. It has been claimed

4. _____ using a hands-free device reduces one type of distraction, it does not eliminate the danger.

   a. While it is true that   b. Of course,   c. It might be claimed that

5. Some researchers have found that talking with a passenger in one's car is just as dangerous as talking on a phone, but _____ .

   a. other researchers disagree   b. it is not true that   c. it has been argued

6. _____ , a passenger can help the driver see danger, while a person at the other end of a phone call cannot.

   a. It could be claimed   b. It is not true that   c. Obviously

7. When it comes to texting and driving, _____ mostly young people are at fault, but research shows that people of all ages are using hand-held devices while driving.

   a. naturally   b. it could be claimed that   c. it is not true that

8. Many people think that they can do two things at once. _____ , that is probably not true.

   a. It is argued that   b. However   c. Some researchers disagree

3 Unscramble the sentences about information overload.

1. lead / important health information / individuals to ignore / information overload can / it is argued that

   It is argued that information overload can lead individuals to ignore

   important health information.

2. in an age with so many / clearly, / we are fortunate to live / sources of good health information

   _____

3. to an increase in good behaviors / can lead to an increase / naturally, / access to information / in awareness and therefore

   _____

4. lead to confusion / of information available online / can actually / however, / the huge volume

   _____

5. good health advice / when people are confused, / it has been argued that / they end up not benefiting from

   _____

6. it's hard to know / there are so many different recommendations about health that / which ones to follow / it has been claimed that

_____

7. one source making one claim / of course, information / and later research claiming the opposite / can be contradictory, with

_____

8. while it is true that / should be accessible to everyone / there is a link between education levels and beliefs about health, / good health information

_____

4 Think of what you have learned online about good health and staying well. On a separate piece of paper, write a short paragraph (four or five sentences) persuading people to practice a healthy habit or stop an unhealthy habit. Use common vocabulary that addresses opposing views.

Avoid Common Mistakes

1 Circle the mistakes.

1. You might be surprised **at the work** librarians **do today** (whether) you haven't visited a

    (a)   (b)   (c)

library lately.

2. A librarian can help you **if** you are wondering **if or not** a source **has the information**

        (a)   (b)   (c)

you need.

3. Librarians respond **to all types of requests** for information, so they usually know

            (a)

weather **or not** a source is reliable.

 (b)   (c)

4. Librarians often **help visitors** **use the Internet** **whether** they are unfamiliar with

        (a)   (b)   (c)

searching for information online.

5. Librarians can help **you figure out** if **or not** a book or website has

         (a)   (b)

what you are looking for.

 (c)

6. Some people wonder **wether** **or not** librarians are still relevant **in today's world**.

       (a)   (b)   (c)

7. In difficult times, local governments sometimes have **to decide** if **or not libraries**

                  (a)   (b)

should be kept open.

 (c)

8. Libraries are critical **whether** we **want modern information tools**

        (a)   (b)

to be accessible to everyone.

 (c)

2 Identify the common mistakes in the sentences. Label each sentence with the type of mistake from the box. If there is no mistake, write *d*. Then correct each mistake.

> a. Remember to use *if*, and not *whether*, to express a condition.
> b. Remember that *or not* can immediately follow *whether*, but it can only appear at the end of a sentence with *if*.
> c. Remember to spell *whether* correctly.
> d. There is no mistake.

> *whether*
> *b* How do you know ~~if~~ or not you are suffering from information overload? _____ To
> (1)   (2)
>
> answer this question, it's a good idea to reflect on weather you frequently feel stressed,
>
> or feel that you can't accomplish anything. _____ You may be suffering from information
>   (3)
>
> overload whether you frequently feel depressed or exhausted from staying in touch
>
> electronically. E-mail can be a real source of anxiety. _____ One agency calculated that
>   (4)
>
> if it averaged all of its incoming e-mails for a single week, its employees received 250
>
> e-mails per person every working day. _____ For each message we receive, we have to
>   (5)
>
> decide if or not it needs an answer, can be deleted, or requires an action. _____ Later, we
>   (6)
>
> wonder weather we might have missed something important by acting so quickly. _____
>   (7)
>
> It's not known whether the constant flow of messages is harmful; some believe that it
>
> makes us unable to focus on important tasks, and makes us less creative. _____ Whether
>   (8)
>
> this has happened to you, you might want to try some time management strategies.
>
> _____ Of course, you might ask yourself whether you would have preferred to live in
> (9)
>
> a time when people had too little information, instead of too much. Most likely, the
>
> answer will be no!

Self-Assessment

Circle the word or phrase that correctly completes each sentence.

1. People need to think about _____ balance social networking websites and real-life situations in a healthy way.

   a. how they can   b. how can they   c. how can

2. _____ social networking websites are 100% safe. However, this is simply not true.

   a. It has been claimed that   b. While it is true that   c. Obviously

3. Corporations want to find out _____ social networking websites will help them attract more customers.

    a. if   b. while   c. can they

4. Some employers want to find out _____ reduce information overload in their employees.

    a. whether can   b. they if   c. how they can

5. Many companies wonder _____ benefit them.

    a. how can technology   b. technology can   c. how technology can

6. Shifts in technology happen quickly; it can be a challenge to know _____ .

    a. what the best choices are   b. what are the best choices   c. the best choices are

7. More research is needed on _____ best be used in the workplace and in education.

    a. how can technology   b. technology can   c. how technology can

8. Individuals need to decide _____ constantly accessible by phone, texts, and e-mail.

    a. what they want to be   b. they want to be   c. whether or not they want to be

9. From time to time, it's a good idea to ask yourself _____ too connected.

    a. if you are   b. whether or not you   c. are you

10. _____ by several researchers that Internet use, like TV watching, contributes to weight gain.

    a. It could be argued   b. It has been argued   c. It has argued

11. _____ we are lucky to live in the information age, it is still a good idea sometimes to just turn everything off and relax.

    a. However,   b. It is not true that   c. While it is true that

12. We depend on _____ and are fortunate to have access to so many sources.

    a. information of course   b. information, of course,   c. information of course,

13. _____ or not we handle information well is up to us.

    a. If   b. Whether   c. Weather

14. _____ you want to post your personal information on social networking websites is your decision, but check the sites' privacy policies before you do.

    a. Unless   b. If   c. Whether or not

15. According to the latest statistics, well over 800 million people in the world have a social networking account. _____ people have embraced this phenomenon.

    a. Possibly   b. Clearly,   c. However,

Persuasion 3
Social Networking

Expressing Future Actions

1 A Complete the sentences about social networking. Use the clues and modal verbs in parentheses. Sometimes more than one answer is possible.

1. Social networking sites *may/might/could lose* users if they continue current practices. (lose; possibility)

2. Advertisements on social networking sites _____ a major issue soon, as users are becoming increasingly irritated by their presence. (become; expectation)

3. In fact, SNSs _____ unless there is less advertising. (disappear; possibility)

4. SNS users _____ viewing advertising messages in the future. (stop; possibility)

5. If social networking sites limit advertising messages, they _____ users. (keep; expectation based on condition)

6. In a recent study, many users reported that they _____ to pay to use SNSs if it would mean fewer ads. (be willing; expectation based on condition)

7. In the same study, a significant number of users said they _____ SNSs if there is less advertising. (visit; possibility)

8. These survey results _____ future advertising campaigns. (affect; expectation)

B Read the sentences in A again. Then answer the question.

Which sentences in A have more than one possible modal? _____ Write them next to the sentences.

2 Circle the words that best complete each sentence.

1. After months of research, we **are about** / **will** to unveil a new marketing plan.

2. We **intend to** / **are about** advertise on only one social networking site.

3. Therefore, we **are going to** / **anticipate** determine which site is the most popular with our potential customers.

4. Research indicates that one site **is going / is considering** to overtake all the other social networking sites in the near future.

5. We **will / anticipate** focusing on that site as opposed to any others.

6. We **will / seem likely** need a variety of ads on this one site.

7. For example, we **are going to / are considering** advertising in social networking games.

8. The reason is that the numbers of players of these online games **are likely / will** to increase dramatically in the near future.

3 Complete the paragraphs with the expressions in the box. Use each expression once. Change the form when necessary.

about	be likely to	due to	~~might be~~	seem likely
anticipate	consider	intend to	plan	

Some teachers think that it *might be* necessary to block students' access to social
(1)

networking sites in the future. However, we feel that teachers need to understand the

power of social networking as an educational tool. It _____ that social
(2)

networking is not going to disappear. In fact, it _____ grow in importance in
(3)

the near future. Therefore, schools should _____ exploiting social networking
(4)

instead of banning it.

We are _____ to unveil several new programs at our school that use
(5)

social networking. We will employ social networking tools in several different ways. For

example, the English department _____ maximize the beneficial aspects of
(6)

social networking for communicating with others. Starting next semester, the instructors

_____ to use blogs for writing assignments. This will motivate students by
(7)

giving them the opportunity to have a range of people view and respond to their work.

Our colleagues are likely to find other ways to use social networking as an educational

tool. In fact, the math department is _____ announce a social networking
(8)

program in a few days. We look forward to these changes and _____ having
(9)

great success with these new programs.

4 Answer the questions. Write sentences that are true for you. Use the expression in bold in your answers.

1. What do you **plan to** study in school?

   I plan to study architecture.

2. What do you **hope to** do after you graduate?

   _____

3. What changes, if any, do you **intend to** make in the near future?

   _____

4. What job would you **consider** doing in the future?

   _____

5. What **are** you **likely to** do when you finish school?

   _____

Common Words and Phrases in Persuasive Writing

1 Complete the sentences about social networking sites and communication. Circle the word that correctly completes each sentence.

1. (**Proponents**)/ **Opponents** of social networking sites argue that these communities strengthen relationships.

2. **Opponents / Advocates** of blogging make the claim that it promotes free speech.

3. It is **true / incomplete** that social networking is a useful tool for communication.

4. The main **argument / problem** used by supporters of social networking is that these communities bring like-minded people together.

5. **Supporters / Opponents** of social media claim that these sites are not good for relationships because they reduce the amount of face-to-face communication that people have.

6. Opponents of social media make the **claim / evidence** that these sites are bad for business because many employees access the sites at work.

7. **Proponents / Opponents** of social networking believe that it is a tool for positive social change.

8. Most parents **estimate / support** increased privacy controls on social media sites.

9. Some experts **advocate / believe** monitoring children's use of social networking.

10. However, others **oppose / argue** supervising their online behavior.

11. Opponents of monitoring **argue / refute** that children have the right to privacy.

12. Ruiz **claims / refutes** the notion that children have the right to privacy.

13. Smith's argument about teenagers and the concept of privacy is **valid / incomplete**. She fails to refer to recent literature on adolescent psychology.

14. Green's argument is unproven because there is **little / true** evidence for his claim.

15. Yee's conclusion is **illogical / better** because it is based on ideas that are not true.

2 Unscramble the words to complete the sentences about students' use of laptops. Then check (✓) the statements that are in favor of students using laptops in the classroom.

___✓___ 1. to / order / take / in / notes

Proponents of the idea claim that some students

need laptops in class _in order to take notes_.

_____ 2. idea / opponents / to / the / of / according

_____ , laptops encourage cheating because students can look up answers.

_____ 3. the / argument / used / that / by / main / proponents / of / idea / the / is

_____ laptops help students with poor organizational skills.

_____ 4. students / laptops / distract / claim / can / the / that

_____ is a common argument used by opponents.

_____ 5. of / the / idea / arguments / of / one / against / main / the

_____ using laptops in class is that students are not paying full attention.

_____ 6. claim / favor / that / idea / people / are / the / in / who / of

_____ laptops help students organize important information.

_____ 7. students / that / the / fact / to / due

Advocates of using laptops in the classroom argue that class time is used more efficiently

_____ can look things up instead of interrupting the teacher.

_____ 8. believe / opponents / that / the / of / idea

_____ students can be distracted by the noise of typing or the light on the screens.

Avoid Common Mistakes

1 Circle the mistakes.

1. The (**claiming**) that social networking sites **could** disappear within the next five years
   (a)   (b)
   is **illogical**.
      (c)

2. The administration **will consider** the **arguing** that social networking **is affecting**
                      (a)   (b)   (c)
   students' grades.

3. **Proponents** of the **claiming** that laptops in the classroom are a disturbance **might**
   (a)   (b)   (c)
   have a good point.

4. **According for** a recent report, a large university **is about to** **require** laptops for all
   (a)   (b)   (c)
   entering students.

5. **It seems likely** that a certain number of students **might not agree** with the **claiming**
   (a)   (b)   (c)
   that using social networking sites leads to lower grades.

6. Students **anticipate** **spending** less time online next semester, **according with** a
            (a)   (b)   (c)
   campus survey.

7. **Proponents** of laptops in the classroom **use** the **arguing** that laptops help students
   (a)   (b)   (c)
   take notes.

8. The **arguing** that parents **can** completely control their children's online access
       (c)   (b)
   is **invalid**.
      (c)

2 Identify the common mistakes in the sentences. Label each sentence with the type of mistake from the box. If there is no mistake, write *d*. Then correct each sentence.

> a. Do not confuse the noun and verb form of *claim*.
> b. Do not confuse the noun and verb form of *argue*.
> c. Remember to use *according to*, and not *according for* or *according with*.
> d. There is no mistake.

SNSs and College

≪ previous | index | next ≫

arguments
b One of the main ~~arguing~~ in favor of social networking sites is that they provide an
(1)

easy way for organizations to communicate with individuals. _____ In fact, according with
(2)

a recent report, over 80 percent of colleges and universities in the United States are using

social networking sites to recruit new students and to keep in touch with former students.

_____ In addition, according to the same study, colleges are now using SNSs as part of
(3)

the admission process. _____ Proponents of using social networking sites for college
(4)

admissions argue that it helps them make decisions when there are many equally qualified

candidates. _____ However, their claiming that this is a useful source of information on
(5)

prospective students is invalid. _____ This is because SNSs often contain false information.
(6)

_____ For example, according for a recent study, people are much more likely to lie online
(7)

than they are in face-to-face contact. _____ According for the study, people feel that they
(8)

can get away with lying online because there is no immediate reaction to the lie, as there

would be in face-to-face communication. _____ Another arguing against the use of SNSs in
(9)

college admissions is that it is impossible to know who the actual author of a site is. _____
(10)

False social networking pages can be created to make false claims and spread incorrect

information about an individual. _____ In fact, according with a survey of admissions
(11)

officers, colleges often receive anonymous links to sites with negative information on other

applicants. _____ Whether these sites are genuine or not, this supports the argument that
(12)

they should not be used in the college admissions process.

Self-Assessment

Circle the word or phrase that correctly completes each sentence.

1. We predict that students' grades _____ once we ban access to SNSs.

   a. consider improving   b. improve   c. will improve

2. Experts predict that the popularity of SNSs _____ grow in the future.

   a. likely   b. will   c. anticipate

3. Students are _____ class time checking SNS updates if we do not block access on campus.

   a. going to spend   b. will spend   c. due to spend

4. Without the ban, teachers _____ have to ban laptops in the classroom if they want students to pay attention.

   a. are likely   b. should   c. would

5. We are confident that the proposed rule _____ discourage students from bringing their laptops to class.

   a. would   b. might   c. seems likely

6. We are sure that spending less time on SNSs _____ improve students' grades.

   a. could   b. might   c. should

7. The college _____ unveil a new policy regarding laptops.

   a. is about to   b. intends   c. anticipates

8. The social networking site _____ creating a new privacy policy in the next few months.

   a. is due to   b. is about to   c. anticipates

9. It _____ that more schools will use social networking for educational purposes.

   a. is like   b. seems likely   c. is likely to

10. The company is _____ monitoring employees' Internet use.

    a. considering   b. anticipates   c. is about to

11. Some parents _____ that children should be supervised while they are online.

    a. intend to   b. believe   c. are in favor of

12. Some parents _____ blocking inappropriate websites.

    a. are in favor of   b. argue   c. claim

13. The _____ that colleges need to use social networking sites to evaluate students is illogical.

    a. claimed   b. claim   c. claiming

14. According _____ a recent report, many colleges are using social networking sites to find new students.

    a. to   b. with   c. for

15. Some educators argue that social networking use is distracting for students, but we disagree with this _____ .

    a. claiming   b. claims   c. claim